~~**DON'T TRUST YOUR SPILL CHECK**~~
~~**DON'T TRUST YOU'RE SPELL CHECK**~~
~~**DON'T TRUSS YOUR SPELL CHECK**~~
~~**DON'T RUST YOUR SPELL CHECK**~~
~~**DON'T TRUST YOU SPELL CHECK**~~
~~**DON'T TRUST YOUR SPELL CZECH**~~

DON'T TRUST YOUR SPELL CHECK
Dean Evans

Don't Trust Your Spell Check: Pro Proofreading Tactics And Tests To Eliminate Embarrassing Writing Errors
By Dean Evans

Disclaimer
This book is designed to provide time-saving strategies, techniques and information in regard to proofreading and copy editing. It does not guarantee success. While every attempt has been made to ensure that the information presented here is correct, the contents of this book are the views of the author and are meant for information purposes only.

Acknowledgements
Where possible, the original sources for any quotes and examples featured in this book are credited in the Appendix.

To all of the tireless production editors and sub-editors that I've worked with, whose infuriating edits have usually made my words better. I salute you.

1. Type some s**t in here please

We all make mistakes. But when you work in publishing, some mistakes can be more embarrassing than others. None more so than publishing a magazine with a heading that reads 'Type some s**t in here please'. In capital letters. That's precisely what happened to *Amiga Format* magazine in the early 1990s. I worked on video game magazines during the same period and this sort of mistake put the fear of God into me.

To understand how a sentence like this can make it into print, past the steely gaze of sub-editors and editors, you need to appreciate how the magazine production process works (and what can go wrong). On small magazines, the spine of the team typically consists of the editor, the art editor (a senior graphic designer) and a production editor (or sub-editor). You add extra graphic designers or writers depending on the size of the magazine, its editorial requirements and its budget.

Raw/unedited copy is generated by in-house writers or comes in from freelance contributors. This raw copy is subbed by the production editor and passed across to the art editor who lays it out as a magazine page using graphic design software like Adobe InDesign.

The page layout then goes back to the production editor for another round of subbing, where words are cut if they overrun or added if the copy is too short for the page. If images are included, they need captions. If extra headings or subheadings are required, they need to be typed in. The page might go back to a writer to fill in some of these blanks.

Finally, the page moves onto the editor who has the final check. If the editor finds any mistakes, he/she corrects them or delegates the responsibility by sending the page back to the production editor. Once these changes are made, the editor has the final sign-off and the art editor turns the pages into PDFs so that they are ready to be sent to the printers.

The process works, albeit constantly squeezed by overhanging deadlines and poor staffing levels. But we all make mistakes. Especially when time is short. 'Type some s**t in here please' is a failure on several levels - a failure by the production editor and a failure by the editor, neither of which typed in a more appropriate replacement or spotted the fruity placeholder before the magazine was sent to print.

The small team was obviously up against it, racing against the clock to get its pages done. It's easy to see how this mistake was missed. Give the page a cursory glance and nothing seems to be missing.

Of course, once you make this sort of editorial clanger, you don't tend to make it again. But it's a harsh way to learn the importance of proofreading. The more permanent your words will be, the more rigorously you should check the spelling and grammar. The bigger the font, the more rigorously you should check the spelling and grammar.

If you proofread properly and take your time, there's no excuse for the New Orleans newspaper headline that read: 'Jets Patriots jumphead goes herey barllskdjf fkdasd fg asdf'. Or the street sign that read 'illegally parked cars will be fine' (instead of 'fined'). And spare a thought for poor Gregorio Iniguez, who was sacked from the Chilean Mint for spelling 'CHIIE' rather than 'CHILE' on his country's 50 peso coins. Worse still, the mistake was made in 2008 and nobody spotted the error for a year.

Who this book is for

If you publish or print words of any kind, then this book is for you. For the last few years, I've worked online. So the proofreading and copy editing info featured in this book is primarily aimed at anyone who runs or works on a blog or website and anyone who is involved with publishing articles.

You might be an Internet 'solopreneur', a lone wolf who writes, edits, formats, checks and publishes your own content. Or you might work for a website, either as a content creator or as a production editor, sub-editor or editor - the person in charge of quality control and tasked to edit/proofread the work produced by your colleagues.

Not you? Maybe you want to self-publish a book on Amazon; check through a student essay or thesis; perhaps error-check a company report? Maybe you're involved in creating a brochure, newsletters, business cards, product packaging or signs? Not you either? What about sending an email, posting a Tweet or updating Facebook? They all involve words. Is everything you've typed recently correct? Are you certain? As we'll see, it's not always easy to spot errors.

Whoever you are, whatever you do, you might not have a proofreading process in place. Or you might already be actively proofreading and want to get better at it. If you publish or print words of any kind, you won't want any mistakes to slip through. You'll want to ensure that what you produce is the best that it can possibly be.

This is especially true if you are printing anything. Mistakes on the web can be corrected and forgotten. You don't have that luxury with print. Print has permanency. Just think how you'd feel if you'd been the sign writer who painted 'SHCOOL' in big white letters on a road when you meant to spell 'SCHOOL'. Or that you'd given the OK to a sign that read 'DRIVE-THRU ENTERANCE'. These are real examples. You'll find more proofreading howlers like these later in this book.

Proofreading is an essential part of the publishing process. The larger the font, the more you should check the words. The more permanent the publication or installation, the more you should check through it for mistakes. You should check and re-check everything you plan to publish until your eyes ache or until the words start to look incorrect and you have to look them up again just to make sure that you're not going crazy. And if you have time for a re-re-check, so much the better.

What this book WON'T teach you

I've not written this book as an exhaustive guide to spelling and grammar. It's not attempting to take you back to school or to confuse you with dangling participles, split infinitives and other English language jargon. Most of us maintain a decent working knowledge of grammar. So while we might know that you don't 'pour' over a book, you 'pore' over one, we don't really need to know that these two words are classed as homonyms, specifically 'homophones'. I don't want to go into that sort of excruciating detail because I don't find these elements of language fun.

This book also won't tell you how to get a proofreading or copy editing job. As far as I'm concerned, effective proofreading is part and parcel of being a writer - submitting or publishing copy that's littered with errors isn't a great way to advertise your skills and get more work. That said, if you apply for a proofreading job, you'll face a proofreading test. This book can certainly help you with that.

Finally, this book doesn't reveal a lazy, magic button system that will ensure everything you ever publish is perfect. I wish there was such a system. The truth is that you won't always catch every mistake. Nor will the next person. It's hard to eliminate every error, especially when you are working on a big project with thousands of words.

Why? Because language is complex. It's not just about catching spelling errors, but spotting contextual anomalies and formatting issues. You won't catch every mistake because you're only human. You're prone to distraction, tiredness and boredom. If there was a way to effectively automate the proofreading process, proofreaders would be out of a job.

What this book WILL teach you

This book isn't just about the mistakes we make when we write, it's also about why we make them and what tactics you can use to spot mistakes before it's too late. I'll be covering the following:

- The difference between proofreading and copy editing
- Why you shouldn't skip the proofreading process
- Why we make mistakes (and how to avoid making them in the future)
- Why you can't trust your spell check
- The common mistakes people make
- How a style guide can help you (and how to create one)
- How to hunt down mistakes like a proofreading pro
- How to improve your concentration and stay focused
- The pros and cons of automated proofreading services

All of this information is glued together with practical tips, checklists, lots of examples, plus advice from real proofreaders. This book is also full of proofreading tests for you to try. There's a boat-load of them: from short passages mined with a cluster of spelling errors, to longer text excerpts, where there's only one grammatical goof to spot. These exercises are a good way to see whether your proofreading skills improve as you go through the book. They also handily illustrate some of the common writing mistakes that I talk about.

And who am I? My name is Dean Evans and I've been a writer, editor, sub-editor and author for over 20 years. I've written millions of words for newspapers, magazines and websites, and checked through just as many.

Of course, the problem with writing a book about proofreading is that you're going to look dumb if you make (and miss) a mistake. There's real pressure to get everything right - every word in the right place, correctly spelt (or should that be 'spelled'?) and grammatically correct. But no matter how many times you read, re-read and re-re-read something, the higher the word count, the higher the chance that an error will slip through. It's hard to balance deadlines with perfection. Something has to give.

So I'm hoping to get my mistake out of the way early by spelling 'accomodate' incorrectly. It has two 'm's. 'Accommodate'. There's a red line underneath the word now as I look at it in the word processor, screaming its wrongness. But I'm going to leave the error in and, fingers crossed, there aren't any more. But if you do find any... well, do me a favour will you? Let me know. Email me at **dean@goodcontentcompany.com** and I'll fix them.

Test your proofreading skills

Before we go any further, try reading through the short text excerpt that follows. See if you can spot the **eight** different mistakes in it. This test first appeared on The Good Content Company website. Some of the errors here will be easy to spot and a simple spell check will catch some of them.

Others are a little trickier and blur the line between proofreading and copy editing. In some publishing processes, the two disciplines are separate. But I'd argue that modern content creation requires a more active combination of the two. This is true whether you're looking at the words in a lengthy book manuscript or the words on a street sign.

— copy starts —
When Apple Corps launched their first iPhone in 2008, it didn't dissappoint. In fact, it immediately captured the collective imagination with a geeky allure driven by Apples slick design, the phone's smart flexibilty and it's inovative multi-touch approach.
— copy ends —

So how did you do? Let's go through the text in two stages. First, we'll tackle the errors from a proofreading perspective...

2. Proofreading vs. copy editing

While Wikipedia's definition of proofreading is accurate, it sounds like something dragged from the 1970s. Proofreading, it says, is "the reading of a galley proof or computer monitor to detect and correct production-errors of text or art. Proofreaders are expected to be consistently accurate by default because they occupy the last stage of typographic production before publication."

A 'galley proof' is essentially an uncorrected version of what your finished content will look like when it's finally printed. The phrase echoes the early days of printing technology, when the words on a page were printed using movable type - cast metal blocks crowned with a single, sculpted letter. Galleys were the metal trays into which these typographical blocks were laid.

Physical proofs are still used in print. Book authors, for example, usually receive a set of uncorrected proofs to check over before their book goes to the printers. It's their last chance to spot any mistakes. Proofs are also useful for anyone working on large print projects, such as a magazine or brochure. Viewing a proof not only allows you to look for typographical errors, but to check for any last-minute layout issues with colour reproduction, spacing and fonts.

One of the modern equivalents of the galley proof is the PDF. At the end of the publishing process, pages will be cranked out as high-resolution PDFs before they are sent over to the printers. Proofreading these PDFs is usually the last opportunity to spot any mistakes.

Digital proofreading is different

But what about working online? If your Content Management System (CMS) has a Preview feature (and most do), this will enable you to see exactly what your content will look like when it's published online. A good Preview option will allow you to see whether your copy fits neatly into the website design; whether paragraphs are too long (or too short); whether the text wraps neatly around images; if there is too much space between your subheadings, and so on.

Returning to the Wikipedia definition above, it also mentions that proofreading should "detect and correct production-errors of text or art." The sort of 'production-errors' that a proofreader is looking for aren't just embarrassing spelling gaffes. Proofreading isn't just a manual spell check. A good proofreader will also hunt down incorrect punctuation, tense and tone errors, missing images, missing information, mismatched captions, inconsistent capitalisation, wayward use of bold/italic emphasis and downright ugly text formatting. It depends on the publication.

For print projects, a proofreader will typically double-check page numbers, page references and chapter numbers; plus highlight any lingering widows (the last line of a paragraph that appears awkwardly at the top of a column) or orphans (a single word on the bottom line of a paragraph or an opening line at the bottom of a column). Working online, a digital proofreader might check that any included links work and that a post is correctly tagged or categorised.

Where proofreading fits into the publishing process

Finally, Wikipedia's definition states that proofreading is considered the "last stage of typographic production before publication". A typical magazine process might look like this:

1. Raw copy
2. First edit/copy edit
3. Page layout
4. Second edit/corrections
5. Proofread
6. Final corrections
7. Publish

While a blogging process might look something like this:

1. First draft
2. Copy edit
3. Optimise
4. Proofread
5. Publish

Proofreading is a final, exhaustive error check, not an extra opportunity to rewrite the content. Traditionally, there's no editorial input during a proof. That's reserved for the copy editing phase, which I'll get onto in a moment.

Proofreading? Why bother?

You might think that life's too short for proofreading. I think that all the time. You might be eager to get your words out there to see what sort of impact they have. Or you might want to play fast and loose with language, keeping an edge to what you do. So what if you've got a few words wrong. People can still understand you. Right?

Proofreading sounds like a lot of hard work. It can be tedious to check and re-check a document, hunting for spelling and grammar errors. It's no wonder people often skip the proofreading process entirely. It's hard to focus on a task that you don't enjoy.

You might avoid proofreading for any number of other reasons. You might not have the time to check your work again due to a pressing deadline. You might proofread too quickly, not focusing on every word and ultimately missing simpler errors. Or perhaps somebody you trust to check your work is guilty of the same thing. If you work online, you might think that you'll spot mistakes later and simply correct them.

If you don't have time to proofread yourself, it might be difficult to justify hiring someone to proofread for you or buying some proofreading software. Getting a second pair of eyes to look over your work is a great idea, but not everybody can afford it.

It's all too easy to devalue proofreading; all too easy to underestimate its impact on how people see you. But it's an important part of the publishing process, whether you're a commercial print publisher, a lone-wolf blogger, or a student writing a thesis or applying for a job.

Despite the popularity of TV, radio, YouTube and podcasting, most communication still uses the written word. Think CVs and covering letters, essays, chat sessions, emails, blog posts, books, posters, brochures and newsletters. Accuracy matters. The words that you write reflect on you or your company. Readers will usually tolerate small mistakes - writing 'teh' in an email when you meant 'the', or missing an 's' off of the end of a word that's buried deep in the text of an article.

But let three, four or more mistakes slip through and your work starts to look shoddy. People can't help but transfer this shoddyness across to the person that wrote it. If your writing and grammar is woeful, it can reflect badly on any services or products that you provide.

The consequences of poorly-written content aren't just limited to embarrassment. In the case of Gregorio Iniguez at the Chilean Mint, he suffered financially, losing his job.

Mitt Romney famously released an app with a photo frame that read "A BETTER AMERCIA", one of a number of damaging spelling errors in his campaign materials. Failing to properly proofread content can not only dent your reputation, it can lose you a job, lose you clients, lose you readers and lose you sales.

Perfectly spelt, formatted and structured content is what people expect. Mistakes suggest a lack of care in your writing, poor quality control, even ignorance. Mistakes get through because you either don't notice them or don't know that they are wrong. A typo can jolt a reader, shifting their attention to focus on an incorrect spelling rather than what you have to say.

You might think that you can trust your spell checker. Why do you need to waste time proofreading when a half-decent word processor will spot mistakes for you in half the time? There are three answers to this.

1. Not everybody does a spell check. Do you religiously spell check everything that you write? And I mean everything? If you update an article or edit a paragraph in a book, do you run a spell check again? Whenever you make changes to content, adding or deleting words, there's the potential for errors to creep in.

2. Not everybody can do a spell check. You might not be in a position to do a spell check. A sign writer, for example, doesn't have access to a spell check nor are spell checks a consistent feature in website Content Management Systems. As for the spell checking functionality in many desktop publishing applications... it leaves a lot to be desired.

3. A spell check won't spot every mistake. Most word processors include spell check functionality that can spot wrongly spelt words, repetition, rogue spaces and some rudimentary grammar problems. But they don't catch everything. A spell check is only as good as its internal dictionary. You might be surprised at how dumb they actually are and how disastrous it can be to rely on them for quality control.

Proofreading disasters

Mistakes are easy to make and the consequences of missing out the proofreading stage can be dire. Consider a recipe printed in an Australian cook book that required 'salt and freshly ground black people' instead of 'salt and freshly ground black pepper'. Wince at the US high school, which advertised 'laeping to literacy night' and pity the new Debenhams store that proudly advertised a grand opening in 'Febuary 2010'.

Nobody is immune to making mistakes. Even the largest companies. A big antivirus software provider was recently spotted offering 'Antitvirus' protection on its website, while a not-so-bright spark at Google forgot to put the month of December 2012 into the Android 4.2 People/Contacts application. As gaffes go, this one was Grand Canyon-sized.

The most common mistakes are simple spelling errors. But you'd be amazed how catastrophic missing out a single letter can be. There's the tattoo artist who inked the phrase 'I'm Awsome' across a customer's back. 'Awesome' work. Or adding extra letters where they don't belong... A mistake made by a Baltimore news channel subtitled the visiting Prince Harry as the 'Prince of Whales' (enormous marine mammals) instead of the 'Prince of Wales' (a small country in the UK).

And who can forget that moment in 1992 when Vice President Dan Quayle wrongly corrected a sixth-grader and forced him to add an 'e' to the end of 'potato'.

Getting a word wrong or missing out a word can also

cause embarrassment. A 1631 edition of the King James Bible missed out the vital word 'not' in one of the 10 Commandments, creating a new one - 'Thou shalt commit adultery'. I also like this apology from an American newspaper, which reads: 'Due to a typing error, Saturday's story on local artist Jon Henninger mistakenly reported that Henninger's band mate Eric Lyday was on drugs. The story should have read that Lyday was on drums.'

Finally, pity poor *Seinfeld* actress Julia Louis-Dreyfus, who turned up to find that her new star on the Hollywood Walk of Fame had beautiful gold lettering that spelt 'Julia Luis Dreyfus'. It was hastily corrected for the ceremony that followed.

There are words in the English language that many of us get wrong on a regular basis. Is it 'indispensable' or 'indispensible'? 'Blatent' or 'blatant'? 'Seperate' or 'separate'? Yes, a spell check will catch any incorrect spellings here (it's 'indispensable', 'blatant' and 'separate'). But sometimes only a proofread will do.

Proofreading test answers

All of which brings us back to that short text excerpt I showed you earlier. Here it is again, this time with six of the eight mistakes highlighted in bold. Did you spot them?

— *copy starts* —
When Apple Corps launched **their** first iPhone in 2008, it didn't **dissappoint**. In fact, it immediately captured the collective imagination with a geeky allure driven by **Apples** slick design, the phone's smart **flexibilty** and **it's inovative** multi-touch approach.
— *copy ends* —

These are the mistakes that a good proofreading pass should catch. In fact, a simple spell check in a word processor such as Microsoft Word should catch four of them.

their: Companies such as Apple are traditionally referred to as singular entities. So this sentence would use 'its first iPhone' rather than 'their first iPhone'. A spell check won't highlight this error, so it's often missed during a text-check.

dissappoint: There's only one 's' in 'disappoint'.

Apples: This word should have an apostrophe – i.e. Apple's. We're talking about the company's 'slick design' here. In other words, the 'slick design' is referencing the word 'company', so it needs a possessive apostrophe to indicate this.

flexibilty: A spelling mistake that can be hard to spot. We're missing a final 'i' at the end of 'flexibility'.

it's: As opposed to the 'Apples' example previously, the wayward use of an apostrophe here turns 'its' into 'it is'. This would make the sentence read: "the phone's smart flexibilty and it is inovative multi-touch approach." Which doesn't make sense. The correct word is 'its' – no apostrophe.

inovative: Another spelling mistake. There are two 'n's in 'innovative'.

Ultimately, a corrected version of this text would read:

"When Apple Corps launched its first iPhone in 2008, it didn't disappoint. In fact, it immediately captured the collective imagination with a geeky allure driven by Apple's slick design, the phone's smart flexibility and its innovative multi-touch approach."

It's better. But it's still not perfect. There are still two errors in it. To find those you step out of the world of proofreading and into copy editing territory...

What is copy editing?

It's important to make the distinction between copy editing and proofreading. Traditionally, the two are very different disciplines. The Wikipedia hive mind describes copy editing as the act of "correcting spelling, punctuation, grammar, terminology, jargon, and semantics, and ensuring that the text adheres to the publisher's style or an external style guide."

There's obviously some crossover here with proofreading. But copy editing is primarily focused on improving content, checking for factual errors and making sure that the copy fits in with the style, tone and editorial approach of the publication. It also takes into account the expectations of the intended audience - what they like, what they don't like; what fits their expectations and what doesn't; what ideas and language they identify with; and so on. A copy edit is where you'll make the most changes to content.

What sort of changes? Copy editing is about taking a messy first draft (aka raw copy) and making sure that it fits in with the style of the publication and that it fulfils a brief/commission and the promise of its headline. It's about chopping out unnecessary words; simplifying language; slicing out rambling introductions and punctuating overlong sentences. Copy editing is also an opportunity to sense-check the content, looking at whether concepts are clearly and fully explained; facts, names and places are correct; jargon is minimised; and that nothing in the copy is libellous or just plain untrue.

A good copy edit will mean that there's almost nothing to catch in a subsequent proofreading pass. But be wary... The worst kind of copy editing makes changes for the sake of making changes. I once had an editor who couldn't help but rewrite everyone's copy, overpowering and diluting the voice of each writer in the process. Good copy editing preserves the original voice but makes it clearer. Copy editing is copy polishing. Proofreading is checking that you haven't missed a bit.

If we look at the short proofreading test again, a good copy edit would ideally catch all eight mistakes. After the proofreading pass, we identified six of them. Here's that corrected excerpt again, this time with the last two mistakes highlighted in bold:

"When **Apple Corps** launched its first iPhone in **2008**, it didn't disappoint. In fact, it immediately captured the collective imagination with a geeky allure driven by Apple's slick design, the phone's smart flexibility and its innovative multi-touch approach."

Apple Corps: This is a factual error. It was Apple Inc (or just 'Apple') that launched the iPhone. Apple Corps is actually the multimedia company founded by The Beatles.

2008: Another fact-checking test. The first iPhone was launched in mid-2007, not 2008.

The two remaining errors are factual and these are the sort of mistakes that are trickier to identify. If you look at the corrections pages in newspapers, you'll see that the majority of errors are factual faux pas like these. Here are a few examples from *The Guardian*'s Corrections and Clarifications page to illustrate what I mean:

"A front-page article on Barack Obama's inauguration referred to him as the 45th, rather than the 44th US president."

"A cracking tale: why did the world's first jetliner fall out of the sky? was amended to clarify that the de Havilland Comet was the first passenger jet, not the first jet. That honour went to the German air force's Heinkel He 178 prototype."

"Zero Dark Thirty: the US election vehicle that came off the rails was amended because the original said: 'Obama and his commanders followed the mission to kill Obama in real time'. This has been corrected to say the mission to kill Bin Laden."

"An article about sales of physical copies of music in the UK said that 3% of the 189m singles sold last year were CDs. This should have said 0.3%."

"The Newcastle footballer pictured in an article about whether Demba Ba would stay at the club was not Ba, but his fellow striker Papiss Cissé."

Some of these aren't the sort of errors that a last-stage proofread would normally pick up. But I'd argue that the modern writer, blogger or author needs to be both copy editor and proofreader, especially if working alone or as part of a small team. You should never take anything at face value and only trust a fact when you can double-check it. But even though newspapers employ dedicated copy editors and proofreaders to catch these types of error, mistakes still get through. The question is why?

There's not a simple answer. Everybody makes mistakes. We're only human. Wherever there is a written word, there is the potential for an error. On the one hand, we need to get better at spotting any mistakes that we've made, catching and eliminating them before publication.

But we can also look at why we make mistakes in the first place and try to make less of them.

3. A proofreader walks into a bar...

A proofreader walks into a bar.

The barman says: "What'll you have sir?"

"First," sighs the proofreader, "it should be 'what will you have', not 'what'll'. That's just bad English. Second, it's madam."

Why do we make mistakes?

In some respects, making mistakes is unavoidable. As you'll see in this chapter, there are so many ways to make them and a variety of factors will affect the quality of what we do.

If you're a writer, you can potentially make fewer mistakes if you know why you're making them. If you're a copy editor or a proofreader, you can improve your error-spotting abilities if you know what mistakes people tend to make and which ones a spell check won't be able to catch.

Catching mistakes is one thing. But why do we make them in the first place? Here are a few observations... For starters, we often litter copy with typos when we type too quickly, trying to get our ideas into words and out onto the page as quickly as possible before we forget them. Messy, error-strewn first drafts are a first step for many writers, including myself.

Errors might also creep in when the high tech writing software we use auto corrects an unfamiliar (but correct) word for something that we didn't mean to write. Modern word processors auto-spell check and auto capitalise, they judge our grammar choices in real time and highlight most mistakes as we type. This can be both a help and a hindrance.

That doesn't mean what you think it means...

We also make errors when we don't know how to use certain words correctly and we have always misused them. Consider the word 'peruse', which you might think means to scan, skim-read or browse. It actually means 'to read thoroughly or carefully'. People often misuse 'unique', which means 'one of a kind' and 'having no like or equal'. So it can't be modified with adjectives like 'very' or 'absolutely'. Something is either unique or it isn't.

We make some errors because we've always misspelled certain words - like writing 'firey' when you should be using 'fiery', or spelling 'apartment' with two 'p's. There are also geographic considerations here. What might not seem a typo to a UK reader ('manoeuvre'), might jolt a reader from the US who is expecting to see the word written as 'maneuver'. Ditto 'spelt' and 'spelled'.

"Sure, I can write about Quantum Mechanics..."

There's a chance that mistakes will be made when we don't fully understand the subject we're writing about or proofreading. Given enough time to get their head around a subject, a good writer should be able to write about anything. Skimp on research, however, and you can easily find yourself making mistakes that you'll never spot because you lack the expert knowledge to know that they're wrong.

We make mistakes when we're too familiar with the words we're checking. It's why it's harder to proofread your own words. You remember writing and rewriting them. So you know what to expect as you re-read them. This intimacy can lead to missing certain errors that a fresh pair of eyes would spot easily, because your brain shows you what you expect to see, not what is actually there on the page.

You can also miss mistakes if the same text is repeated multiple times. When you've read text once, you might not give it your full attention when it appears again. I remember subbing through a football guide that had a section devoted to the Champions League finals between 1993 and 2012. Each one had a small fact box, which featured three consistent elements - the date of the final, the name of the football stadium where the final was played, and the match attendance.

With 19 matches, that meant 19 fact boxes, each one repeating similar information, like 'Attendance: 87,000', 'Attendance: 47,875', and so on. It's easy to start focusing on the text that changes each time - the attendance figure - when you should be checking the whole phrase, including the word 'attendance'. Which is why I almost missed that three of the fact boxes featured the word 'attendence'. Almost...

The unlucky editor

We make mistakes when we try to correct existing mistakes. If you edit a sentence to rewrite it, there's always the possibility that any new text that you drop in could have an error in it, or that it doesn't fit in with the rest of the copy. When you edit, you typically change words and move on. But it's important to re-read any sentence or paragraph that you've edited to make sure that there are no new gaffes or that, by concentrating on one mistake, you failed to spot another one close by.

We make mistakes when we're pressed for time. Think how you read when time is short. You often find yourself skipping over words, gleaning the meaning without noticing the construction of the words themselves. Again, you assume rather than properly check and when you do this you'll often miss the simplest mistakes. There's danger in a cursory glance. It satisfies the need for checking something and ticks the proofreading box. But you either proof something properly or you don't. A cursory glance isn't enough, it's a check driven by obligation rather than dedication; by speed rather than process.

"Ooh, a bird…"

Crucially, we make mistakes when we are distracted. Research suggests that even small distractions, such as reading a text message or glancing at an email, can have a huge effect on your ability to complete a task quickly. When we focus on a single task at the exclusion of all others, we can slip into a flow state. Athletes often call it 'the zone'. But when we switch between tasks there's a performance/productivity cost for doing so. Have you ever stopped what you were doing to answer an email or talk on the telephone, only to ask yourself: 'now where was I?' It usually takes you a few minutes to get going again. Increase the number of distractions or tasks and mistakes can creep in and real productivity takes a nose-dive.

The multitasking myth

Multitasking is usually to blame. In the 1990s, the concept was all the rage as office workers embraced immediacy and juggled several tasks at once, such as writing a report, talking on the phone, answering emails and sending text messages. The modern equivalent is having eight web browser tabs open, regularly checking Facebook and switching between multiple applications. Multitasking makes you feel more productive and that you're working harder (and smarter) than somebody who is concentrating on a single task.

But Zheng Wang, assistant professor of communication at Ohio State University, believes that this is a myth. People misperceive the positive feelings they get from multitasking, he argues. "They are not being more productive - they just feel more emotionally satisfied from their work."

That's the danger. According to Wang's research, trying to concentrate on something else as you work or study makes you less effective. In an example from Ohio State University's multitasking research, students who watched TV whilst reading a book reported feeling more satisfied than those who didn't watch TV. But crucially, those who watched TV reported that they "didn't achieve their cognitive goals as well." Subconsciously, if you perceive a task as boring (and you rather not be doing it), you'll often try to introduce something to make the task more entertaining. It's yet another reason why we're prone to distraction.

You can't multitask. You really can't

You might think that you can multitask effectively, especially if you write or proofread with music on. But listening to music is a low-intensity task. It doesn't require any concentration or ask the brain to process anything. The truth is, you can't effectively juggle more than two intensive tasks at the same time.

Etienne Koechlin and Sylvain Charron of the French biomedical research agency INSERM in Paris suggest that we struggle to cope with three or more things because our brains only have two hemispheres available for handling tasks. "In terms of everyday behaviour, you can cook and talk on the phone at the same time," Koechlin explained in *Science Now*. "The problem arises when you pursue three goals at the same time. Your prefrontal cortex will always discard one."

It should come as no surprise to learn that we tend to make mistakes when we're tired. Writing requires a degree of concentration, a flow that smoothly channels the words in your head down through your fingers on the keyboard and into the word processor of your choice. Work late or spend too long at the keyboard and this flow begins to stutter and stop. Your eyes begin to glaze over. Your mind wanders. Sentences become harder to write, simple words get misspelt, your language devolves and you find yourself deleting and retyping... deleting and retyping as your fingers just won't obey orders from your brain.

Finally, we also make mistakes when we're bored. It's hard to concentrate fully on a task that you have no interest in or passion for.

How to avoid making mistakes

If you're a writer who also proofreads, then making improvements in some or all of these areas means you'll potentially make fewer mistakes and spend less time proofreading. Treat a quickly-written first draft as the messy, error-strewn brain-dump that it is. When you've finished writing it, dedicate some copy editing time to bang it into shape. Some things to remember...

Don't blindly trust a spell checker. As we've already seen, a spell checker can catch most spelling errors and some grammatical problems. But it's not a replacement for reading and re-reading your work carefully before you print or publish.

Write simply and clearly. There's no need to demonstrate your language knowledge by using flamboyant or flowery wordage. The most effective way to communicate with someone is to keep it simple. If you're unsure about a word, look it up. Keep a dictionary next to you as you write or bookmark dictionary.reference.com.

Write what you know (where possible). If somebody asked me to write about quantum mechanics, I might be tempted to give it a go. I'm sure there's a cat involved somewhere... But it's not my area of expertise and, chances are, my lack of knowledge on the subject would show through in my writing. However, ask me to write about mobile phones, then I'm your guy. You can minimise errors when you write about subjects that you know well. If you do find yourself tasked with an unfamiliar subject, seek advice from experts and interview or quote them.

Write when you're most productive. Everyone has a time when they are at their most productive. For me, it's in the morning. On a good day, I can get 1,000-2,000 words written per hour. My productivity decreases in the afternoon, and I've recently abandoned writing in the evening, where I don't seem to be able to manage more than 250-500 words and even that is a painful struggle. When you feel yourself getting tired, stop. When you feel your enthusiasm waning, stop. Take a break and come back to it.

Make yourself comfortable. Work in an environment that helps rather than hinders the writing process. Minimise distractions. Work with headphones on. Or without. Whatever works for you. Turn your phone off. Turn the Internet off. To avoid stopping to make several cups of tea or coffee, make a flask. Not every tactic will work for you. Experiment until you find what does.

Fight the urge to cut corners. We might skip over words in a sentence, telling ourselves that they're fine, that we've read them before and they haven't changed. But once you cut a corner and convince yourself that it's OK to do so, it gets easier to tell yourself the same thing next time. Your reward is finishing the task sooner. But you could miss errors for the sake of speed.

Don't write things at the last minute. Give yourself

enough time to get your project done. Of course, you might work well when the clock is ticking and you're up against it. But speediness has its drawbacks. You cut corners. You abandon perfection in pursuit of completion.

Finally, and crucially, by understanding and recognising the common mistakes we can make, you can learn to avoid them.

Proofreading test #2

Here's another test. Can you find the mistake(s) in this excerpt from an article about the 150th anniversary of the London Underground? This is a proofreading challenge, not a copy editing one, so be on the look out for spelling errors and incorrect punctuation. The answers follow...

— copy starts —
Oxford Circus is the lynchpin of the Central line. At Ongar, they told me that during the battle to save their station from the cost-cutters they had commissioned a report by accountants Coopers & Lybrand which sought to prove that Oxford Circus was the least productive station on the line because, while it was a destination for thousands, no one bought tickets there. With such statistical sophistry, I can see why their campaign failed

Above ground, Oxford Circus teems. Everyone is selling something. Chuggers energetically chug in the rain; a woman from an eastern religious sect is offering an instant pathway to the Truth; the Topshop sale is pedalling its own version of nirvana; a man next to one of the station's many exits is holding up large placards proclaiming a royal-inspired masonic conspiracy. All this hucksterism infects the Central line.
— copy ends —
From: http://www.guardian.co.uk/uk/2013/jan/09/london-

underground-150-years-birthday (page since corrected)

Proofreading test #2 - Answers

Did you spot the typo? There are a few words in this passage that could distract you from the hunt if you haven't encountered them before. 'Lynchpin', for example, can also be spelt 'linchpin' and 'Ongar' refers to Chipping Ongar in the English county of Essex. 'Chuggers' is short for 'charity muggers' and describes a particular breed of street fundraisers who try to wheedle donations out of passers-by. In fact, there's just the one error in this test. It's marked up in bold and shown in the text below.

— copy starts —
   Oxford Circus is the lynchpin of the Central line. At Ongar, they told me that during the battle to save their station from the cost-cutters they had commissioned a report by accountants Coopers & Lybrand which sought to prove that Oxford Circus was the least productive station on the line because, while it was a destination for thousands, no one bought tickets there. With such statistical sophistry, I can see why their campaign failed
   Above ground, Oxford Circus teems. Everyone is selling something. Chuggers energetically chug in the rain; a woman from an eastern religious sect is offering an instant pathway to the Truth; the Topshop sale is **pedalling** its own version of nirvana; a man next to one of the station's many exits is holding up large placards proclaiming a royal-inspired masonic conspiracy. All this hucksterism infects the Central line.
— copy ends —

pedalling: The correct word should be 'peddling'. Pedalling means to use pedals - you 'pedal' a bicycle. The author of this article meant to write 'peddling', which means 'to distribute or dispense'. This error has since been corrected in the published copy. The confusion arose because 'pedal' and 'peddle' are homophones. These, and many other mistakes, are covered in the next section.

What mistakes do we make?

Language is changing, evolving. Or in some cases, it's devolving, reduced to a string of short codes and WTF acronyms. Is that wrong? No. If you're a writer, how you use language is part of your unique voice and you can bend old literary rules as you see fit. You can have short sentences. Like this. Start new paragraphs with 'And', 'Because' or 'But'. You don't have to hold off using the word 'decimate' because it technically means 'to reduce by one tenth'. You can even make up words in fits of joyous word makeupery...

Writers should experiment. Play. Bend the rules. That's half the fun of writing. But spell 'rhythm' incorrectly or put an apostrophe in DVDs and you can look like a fool.

How does this help a copy editor or proofreader? Knowing the sort of common mistakes that people make can help you spot them. Knowing that writers might miss out the second 'i' when they write 'liaison' or have problems telling the difference between 'they're', 'their' and 'there' can help you be extra vigilant when these words appear. Errors will range in severity, from the annoying spoiler (the one tiny mistake that spoils your content) to the shameful clanger (when you should really know better) and the embarrassing howler (the sort of mistake that makes you want to curl up into a ball and die...)

Over the following pages, you'll find a rundown of the most popular grammatical goofs and gaffes, including spelling errors, inconsistencies and wayward captions. Let's start with some basic errors that should be easy to spot...

Your or You're?
'Your' and 'you're' are often misused in sentences and they can be easy to miss during a proofreading session, especially if you like to say the words aloud to yourself as you read. As far as language rules go, 'your' is possessive, indicating something that belongs to you - i.e 'your hat' or 'your coat'. While 'you're' is short for 'you are'. Here are a few examples:

- Is eating lunch at your desk bad for you?
- Google reads all your emails
- 6 mobile security screw-ups you're (probably) guilty of
- You're kidding, right?

Will a spell check catch this error? Mostly. Substituting the opposite word was caught in three of the four examples here when spell checked in Microsoft Word. However, this one, 'Google reads all you're emails', slipped through unnoticed. Shame on you Microsoft Word, shame on you.

Why do people get these words wrong? Words like 'your' and 'you're'; 'who's' and 'whose; or 'they're' and 'their' sound the same, but have different spellings and meanings. They're classed as 'homophones'.

Who's or Whose?
Simply put, 'who's' is the shortened form of 'who is' or 'who has'; 'whose' is possessive. The easiest way to know which one to use is to see whether you can use 'who is' or 'who has' and not lose the sense of the sentence. Here are a few examples that show the two in action:

- Who's in charge of the charity sector?
- 'EU shouldn't define who's a journalist': union says
- Gov renominates judge whose past bid ended in

firestorm
- Whose water is it, anyway?
- The Scottish aristocrat whose pioneering photography drew admiration from Lewis Carroll

Will a spell check catch this error? Yes. And no. Flushing these examples through Microsoft Word, with 'who's' substituted for 'whose' (and vice versa), resulted in a surprising number of misses, including 'Who's water is it anyway?' and 'Gov renominates judge who's past bid ended in firestorm'. This is precisely why you can't trust a spell check...

Its or It's?
'Its' without an apostrophe is possessive - 'its best interests', 'its key features', and so on. Like 'your' and 'you're' and 'whose' and 'who's', 'it's' is the shortened version of 'it is' or 'it has'. With this in mind, it's easy to get the correct usage by reading 'it's' in the long form. Examples below:

- Why it's the right time to buy a second hand motorbike
- [Why **it is** the right time to buy a second hand motorbike - correct]
- How Russia has changed since it's last Olympic Games
- [How Russia has changed since **it is** last Olympic Games - wrong]

It should be: 'How Russia has changed since its last Olympic Games.' Here are some more examples:

- Vienna Opera Ball set to party like it's 1899
- Online radio service TuneIn launches its redesigned web presence

- It's been the best thing I have done

Will a spell check catch this error? For the most part, yes. Although Microsoft Word didn't spot 'Vienna Opera Ball set to party like its 1899'.

They're or Their or There?
Three more words that sound the same, but are spelt differently and have different meanings. Homophones again. In this case, 'their' is possessive - i.e. 'belonging to them'. 'They're' is the shortened form of 'they are', while 'there' refers to a place, i.e. 'here and there', 'there is' and 'there are'. You'll find examples of each below for reference:

- Indian investors are forcing Ethiopians off their land
- What every parent should know before buying their kids a smartphone
- Airport officials say they're ready for Friday's storm
- They're just lifelong best friends
- Is there water on Mars?
- "I might even have the chance to play in a game over there."

Will a spell check catch this error? Again, it can be hit and miss so don't rely on a word processor to do your proofreading for you.
    The built-in spell checkers in Microsoft Word and Google Drive didn't catch the incorrect sentence: 'What every parent should know before buying they're kids a smartphone'. Or this grammatical gaffe: 'There just lifelong best friends'. You have been warned.

To or Two or Too?
Three words, three very different uses. But you can often

find them used incorrectly in sloppy copy. 'Too' means 'more than enough' or 'excessively'. 'To' is typically used with verbs, I.e. 'to do something', but it also means 'toward'. Lastly, 'two' indicates the number 2. For the sake of consistency, you should spell a number out in full when writing 0-9 in text, I.e. 'one', 'two', 'three', and so on. Whereas numbers 10 and above are usually written numerically, I.e. 20, 200, 2,000.

Here are the three words in action:

- Are we too scared, or not scared enough?
- Spain prove too strong for Uruguay in the game
- New theatre to rise at site of Shakespeare playhouse
- Ecoguards on patrol to protect Africa's forest elephants
- Why is the President going to Israel?
- British troops to be sent to Somalia as military commitment spreads
- France make two changes for Wales match in Paris
- A tale of two brothers who took diving to new depths

Will a spell check catch this error? You'd hope so, but again the spell check in the average word processor is dumber than a box of spanners. Try typing this one in: 'British troops two be sent to Somalia as military commitment spreads'. Your spell check probably won't notice the mistake.

Over the next few pages, you'll find some more homophone examples that are often used incorrectly by writers, either accidentally (because they are writing too fast) or because they don't know the difference between the two words.

Whether or Weather?
'Whether' is an expression of doubt - 'I'm not sure whether I

believe him'. 'Weather' is a description of atmospheric conditions - 'The weather outside is frightful'

Enquire or Inquire? (Enquiry or Inquiry?)
Both forms of this verb are correct. You'll find 'enquire' and 'enquiry' used in British English, while 'inquire' and 'inquiry' are often used in US English. Whichever version you use, make sure that the usage is consistent throughout a document.

Program or Programme?
In US English, 'program' can mean a 'plan of action', 'a schedule of activities', a 'TV show' or a computer application. In British English, however, 'program' is only used when talking about computer programming - 'The program crashed, so John had to restart it'. The alternate spelling 'programme' is used to describe plans, schedules and shows. When used as a verb, the only spelling is 'program' - 'Mark Zuckerberg started to program Facebook while he was an undergraduate at Harvard'.

License or Licence?
If you're writing for a US audience, you use the word 'license' as a noun ('he was granted a license') and the same word doubles up as a verb ('he planned to license the technology and make a fortune'). British usage is slightly more fiddly as the noun is spelt 'licence'. So the earlier example becomes - 'he was granted a licence'.

Principle or Principal?
While these two words sound the same, their definitions couldn't be more different. On the one hand, 'Principle' typically means 'a rule or belief' or 'a fundamental truth' - 'it was a matter of principle', 'Republicans interested in power, not principle'. On the other hand, 'principal' means 'the highest in rank' - 'he was the principal player in the biggest

federal scandal for decades'. As a noun it can describe a 'chief' or 'head' of an organisation - 'he was happy to take over as the school's principal'.

Cite, Sight or Site?

A trio of homophones that can confuse rookie writers and using the wrong one can be embarrassing. The primary definition of 'cite' is 'to quote' - 'he cited problems such as violent crime and food shortages'. But it can also mean 'to summon to court' - 'the driver was cited after hitting a patrol car'. 'Sight', meanwhile, can mean 'a view' ('that's a beautiful sight'), 'the act of seeing' ('it was love at first sight'), 'the range of seeing' ('there's no end in sight for the Syrian humanitarian crisis'), even a 'gun sight'. Lastly, 'site' is a noun that means 'position' or 'specific location' - 'this is the perfect site for a new school', 'burial site' or 'building site'. It's also an accepted truncation of 'web site'.

Don't believe that people can get these words wrong? Neither did I until I saw an itv.com headline that blared: 'City centres 'no go' areas for blind and partially sited'. Oh dear. The word this headline needed was 'sighted'. This isn't just a writing fail. It's also a catastrophic proofreading fail.

Elicit or Illicit?

'Elicit' is to 'draw out or bring out' - 'despite several attempts to elicit a response, I never received one'. 'Illicit', meanwhile, means 'illegal or not permitted' - 'the use of illicit drugs in sport was significantly higher than first thought'.

Ensure or Insure?

Two more sound-a-like words that you might find hiding in sentences where they don't belong. 'Ensure' is to 'make certain or guarantee' - 'six tips to ensure success on the football field'. While 'insure' is to 'guard against loss or harm' - 'the five most expensive cars to insure'.

Complement or Compliment?

These two words can trip up even experienced writers. There's a one letter difference between them. 'Complement' means to 'make complete or perfect' or 'a complete number', while 'compliment' is an 'expression of admiration, kindness or praise'. To 'compliment' someone is to 'praise or congratulate'. Check out the examples that follow.

- The new factory will complement the two existing buildings in Texas
- He had a full complement of soldiers for the assault
- The unexpected compliment from his boss brightened David's mood
- Here, have this complimentary copy of our magazine

Will a spell check catch this error? Mostly. The spell check in Microsoft Word didn't bat an eyelid at the wrongly-written phrase: 'The unexpected complement from his boss brightened David's mood'. But Google Drive spotted it. If there's a lesson here (and if you have time), it's to run your text through different word processors to double-check your spellings.

Practice or Practise?

These words often cause writers to pause in mid-sentence, wondering which one they should be using. It's actually fairly simple. 'Practice' is the noun - 'David went to diving practice at the weekend', while 'practise' is a verb - 'David wanted to practise his diving at the weekend'. In short, you 'practise' diving, you go to diving 'practice'. That said, in the US you can get away with using 'practice' for both noun and verb.

Will a spell check catch this error? No. Try typing in 'you practice diving' and 'you go to diving practise'. Neither will cough up an error in a typical word processor.

Council or Counsel?
When words sound the same, there is always the potential for error. 'Council' refers to an 'assembly', ('the council made the decision to cut funding'). While 'counsel' is another word for 'advice', ('after seeking the counsel of his colleagues, he proposed a funding cut'). Note that 'counsel' can also be used as a verb.

Will a spell check catch this error? Yes. And no. Rewrite the previous sentence as 'the counsel made the decision to cut funding' and neither Microsoft Word or Google Drive protested. Swapping 'counsel' for 'council' in the second of our examples didn't escape the spell check's low-IQ gaze, however.

Prophesy or Prophecy?
Like 'practise' and 'practice', the difference between these two words is that 'prophesy' is the verb ('to predict the future') and 'prophecy' is the noun ('a prediction for the future').

Will a spell check catch this error? Yes.

Stationary or Stationery?
More homophones, differentiated by a single letter and easy for some writers to mix up unintentionally. 'Stationary' means 'without moving' - 'The traffic was stationary. It hadn't moved for ten minutes'. While 'stationery' refers to 'writing paper' - 'David ordered his personalised stationery the next day'.

Advice or Advise?
You 'advise' someone, you give 'advice'. For example, 'I would advise you to get some insurance' and 'If somebody told you to get insurance, that's good advice'.

Affect or Effect?
Some people struggle to tell the difference between these two words and you can often find the wrong one used in articles by mistake. 'Affect' means 'to influence or change' and is mostly used as a verb - 'The illness would not affect his grade scores'. While 'effect' is usually a noun and is the result of a change - 'The illness had no effect on his grade scores'. Of course, the worldly-wise amongst you will know that 'effect' can also be used as a verb. In this case it means 'to bring about or make happen'. For example - 'Chilean guitarist uses music to effect change'. Watch out for 'effect/affect' errors in this sense.

Loose or Lose?
Writers can often mix up these two words. 'Lose' is a verb that means 'to be deprived of or cease to have or retain (something)' - 'do not lose the dogs' and 'if we don't score soon, we will lose the game'. 'Loose' is an adjective, defined as 'free of anything that restrains or binds' - 'the dogs are loose', 'do you have any loose change?', 'these trousers are a bit loose around the waist'.

I or me?
Is it 'The King and I'? Or should it be 'The King and Me'? Knowing whether to use 'I' or 'me' in a sentence can also be confusing. It's not an embarrassing mistake if you get it wrong, but it's good to know the rule. See if you can tell which one of the following sentences is correct.

- David wants to invite you and I to go on holiday with him.
- David wants to invite you and me to go on holiday with him.

It's the second one - 'you and me'. Did you get it right? 'I' is generally used when it is the subject of the sentence, 'me' is used when it is the object of the sentence. Here is an example of where 'I' works in the sentence: 'You and I should go on holiday with David'. The 'I' in this example is the subject, while David is the object.

Will a spell check catch this error? Actually, yes. Microsoft Word pointed out the grammatical error in 'David wants to invite you and I to go on holiday with him'.

Less or Fewer?
This is another potentially tricky one, which can have you reaching for the dictionary. 'Less' is used with things that cannot be counted or represented as a number. Something that is just amorphous 'stuff'. Like custard. You should use 'fewer' when there is a definite number of things that can be visualised. Check out the examples below:

- I would like to do less work this week
- I would like to do fewer days of work this week
- He had less money than his brother
- He had fewer coins in his pocket than his brother

Will a spell check catch this error? No. You can switch around fewer and less in the examples above and a spell check will be none the wiser. Even though 'I would like to do fewer work this week' is so stunningly wrong, it hurts my head to write it down...

Like or As?
Two more words that, when wrongly used, can sneak past everyone apart from the dedicated proofreader.

Technically, it's wrong to say: 'It looks like it is going to rain'. But right to say: 'It looks as if it is going to rain'. Of course, you can play fast and loose with this grammatical rule. Fingers crossed, nobody is going to pull you up on a misplaced 'like'. But if you want rules, you can have rules. Firstly, you shouldn't use like before a verb. 'Like' is a comparison:

- He soared through the air like a bird
- He felt good, this was just like the old days

'Like' also appears in lists: 'The smartphone boasts features like a 4.7-inch screen, 32GB of storage and 3G'. But it's more accurate to say: 'The smartphone boasts key features such as a 4.7-inch screen, 32GB of storage and 3G', or 'The smartphone boasts key features including a 4.7-inch screen, 32GB of storage and 3G'.

Will a spell check catch this error? No. This is one of those rules that can be broken with wild abandon.

Which or That?
Now you might think that these two words are simply interchangeable. Like this:

- The bench was situated on top of a hill that overlooked a picturesque valley
- The bench was situated on top of a hill, which overlooked a picturesque valley

And you'd be right. 'Which' and 'that' effectively glue two clauses together, each one starting a second clause that expands on information mentioned in the first clause. As a link between the two clauses, the example here could be written as two separate sentences. Like this: 'The bench was situated on top of a hill. It overlooked a picturesque valley.' As you'll see, the difference between the two is that when you use 'which', you need to follow it with a comma. Using 'that' doesn't require one.

Will a spell check catch this error? Yes. Even Microsoft Word's built-in spell check will give you a nudge and point out misuse.

May or Might?

Like 'which' and 'that', these two words are mostly interchangeable. Originally, 'may' was the present tense form ('She may stay in a hotel on the coast'), while 'might' was used when describing something in the past tense ('She might have stayed in a hotel on the coast'). But in modern usage, you can swap them around:

- She might stay in a hotel on the coast
- She may have stayed in a hotel on the coast

May/might can also be used in a different context when seeking permission. I.e. 'may I have some tea'. But unless you're writing a period drama like *Downton Abbey*, this shouldn't apply.

Whether or If?

Here's another test for you. Which one of these two sentences is correct?

- We don't know whether they are coming tomorrow
- We don't know if they are coming tomorrow

In this case you can use either, but there are certain times when using 'whether' is preferable. It should be used before 'to' ('I don't know whether to drive today') and we use whether with 'or', especially in 'whether [something] or [something else]' phrases. Examples below.

- I don't know whether to drive today or tomorrow
- He wondered whether he would live or die

Farther or Further?

These two words can often cause confusion. Which one do you use? Further? Farther? The simple answer is that you can use both, even if one of the examples below doesn't sound quite right.

- He couldn't run any further
- He couldn't run any farther
- Farther to the north, the authorities were preparing for a big snowstorm
- Further to the north, the authorities were preparing for a big snowstorm

Of course, watch out for the alternative meaning of 'further', i.e. to 'further his career.' Using 'farther' isn't applicable in this case.

Could Of, Would Of, Should Of
Writing any of these phrases is wrong. We might say 'I could of been a contender...' But that's not how it should be written. If you see 'could of', replace it with 'could have', ('I could have been a contender...'). Ditto 'would of' should be written as 'would have' and 'should of' becomes 'should have'. Fortunately, a spell check should highlight these errors.

To or And?
What's wrong with this sentence: 'Hopefully, we can try and minimise distractions and teach new methods to the people who really matter'? The grammar police would point out that it should be 'try to', not 'try and'.

Other mistakes we make

These aren't the only errors that crop up in raw copy. Be alert for other common mistakes, such as spelling errors, nonsensical sentence constructions, missing captions, formatting errors and inconsistencies. Take a look at the examples that follow...

Missing simple spelling errors

Be on the lookout for words that are regularly misspelt by writers. These will vary depending on subject matter, but they might include:

- Indispensable - often written as 'indispensible'
- Liaison - people often miss out the second 'i'
- Noticeable - you might see it without the middle 'e'
- Blatant - often written as 'blatent'
- Committed - double 'm' and double 't'
- Relevant - not 'relevent'
- Rhythm - not 'ryhthm' or 'rythm'
- Separate - often spelt 'seperate'
- Guarantee - only one 'r'
- Hierarchy - look out for 'heirarchy'
- Fiery - not 'firey'
- Fluorescent - often written without the 'o'
- Manoeuvre - English spelling, US spelling is 'maneuver'
- Perseverance - not 'perserverence'
- Threshold - one 'h'
- Withhold - two 'h's

Ignoring nonsensical sentences

Do all of your sentences make sense? Or is there a hidden meaning? Watch out for unintentional 'dangling modifiers'. Consider this sentence: 'They could see elephants striding across the plain with their binoculars.' The author obviously means that they could see elephants 'through' their binoculars. But as it's written here, it sounds like they could see elephants who were carrying binoculars. Unlikely. Here's another one. 'We saw lots of elephants on vacation'. Again, the author means to say that they saw elephants 'while' they (including the author) were on their vacation. But in its original form, the sentence can also be interpreted in a different (and nonsensical) way: 'seeing vacationing elephants'.

It's easy to focus on hunting for spelling and grammar to such an extent that you forget to check if a sentence makes sense. Consider these real-world newspaper headlines and see if you can spot why they are spectacularly wrong:

- Diana was still alive hours after she died
- Statistics show that teen pregnancy drops off significantly after age 25
- One-armed man applauds the kindness of strangers

Forgetting to check captions
Proofreading isn't just about being on the lookout for errors in the main text of content. Don't forget to check text that appears elsewhere - page numbers, pull-out quotes, annotations and picture captions. Mistakes might not be immediately obvious.

Letting formatting errors slide
Not all errors are spelling or punctuation errors. Sometimes formatting errors will sneak through the content-checking process - double spacing between words; the wrong word emphasised *with* bold or italics; a word that isn't completely formatted in **bold** or it*alics*; an Internet link that is cut off halfway through the URL; a header or a caption that uses the wrong font or is written in the wrong font size.

Sentences that run and run and...
Sometimes it's simple punctuation errors that stand out like sentences that don't have any commas in them so you can't pause for breath much like this sentence that just keeps on going and going and doesn't feature any helpful punctuation at all except for a couple of apostrophes and the full stop that's coming right about now.

Not spotting inconsistencies

A good proofreader will also spot any lingering inconsistencies in content, like talking about 'Janette' in one paragraph, but talking about 'Janet' in another (when it's clearly the same person). Or specifying an acronym first as Long Term Evolution (LTE) and misspelling it later as LET. Consistent spelling is also important. Is it 'cooperation' or 'co-operation'? 'E-mail' or 'email'?

Other inconsistencies are more subtle - the same number might be written in different ways (2000, 2,000, two thousand); date and time formats might differ (4pm, 4.00pm, 4:00pm, 16:00; 23rd January 2013, 23 January 2013, January 23 2013); and page references can vary (p8, p.8, page 8). See if you can spot the inconsistencies in the following text excerpt:

— copy starts —

See Treasurer's House at night as it's transformed with sound effects, colourful lights and intriguing stories in the fourth year of this popular city-wide event on 4 November, from 6.30 - 8pm. Or why not join our friendly team at Hampton Court on the 9th November to learn more about the royal history of this famous English house. You can enjoy demonstrations in the Drawing Room and conservation tours all day, starting from 10:00. Finally Arlington Court is hosting its 2nd Christmas Fair from November 17-18, featuring traditional arts and crafts plus family entertainment all weekend. (Note: for Treasurer House tickets, please book in advance).

— copy ends —

How did you get on? Take a look at this excerpt again, this time with the inconsistencies highlighted in bold.

See Treasurer's House at night as it's transformed with sound effects, colourful lights and intriguing stories in the fourth year of this popular city-wide event on 4 November, from 6.30 - 8pm. Or why not join our friendly team at Hampton Court on the **9th November** to learn more about the royal history of this famous English house. You can enjoy demonstrations in the Drawing Room and conservation tours all day, starting from **10:00**. Finally Arlington Court is hosting its **2nd** Christmas Fair from **November 17-18**, featuring traditional arts and crafts plus family entertainment all weekend. (Note: for **Treasurer House** tickets, please book in advance).

9th November: If we take the early mention of '4 November' to be a stylistic choice, then this should read '9 November'.

10:00: Again, earlier in the text, we've established that the time format is '6.30 - 8pm', so the time should be corrected to '10am'.

2nd: Having allowed 'fourth year' in the first sentence, this reference should be rewritten to say 'second Christmas Fair'. Or you might judge that 'fourth' is wrong and want to replace it with '4th'. This would make '2nd' correct.

November 17-18: Another date inconsistency. The dates should appear before the month.

Treasurer House: This is inconsistent with the earlier spelling, 'Treasurer's House'.

Spelling inconsistencies can also arise with British English and US English spelling. For example, British English words ending in 'our' become 'or' in US English - 'colour' and 'color'. Words ending in 're' become 'er' - 'meagre' (British) and 'meager' (US), 'centre' (British) and 'center' (US). Similarly, words ending in 'ise' become 'ize' - 'organise' (British) and 'organize' (US), 'realise' (British) and 'realize' (US). While words ending in 'ogue' become 'og' - 'dialogue' (British) and 'dialog' (US), 'catalogue' (British) and 'catalog' (US).

There are other key differences. Words that include an 'ae' or 'oe' in British English often become just 'e' in US English - 'archaeology' and 'archeology', for example. Or 'encyclopaedia' (British) and 'encyclopedia' (US). Plus some words that feature double 'l's in British English have single 'l's in US English, such as 'modelling' (British) and 'modeling' (US), 'travelling' (British) and 'traveling' (US). British English spelling also adds an e before '-able' - see 'likeable' and 'likable', 'sizeable' and 'sizable'; while words ending in '-ence' often become 'ense' in US English. The classic example is 'defence' (British) and 'defense' (US).

If your content is aimed at a specific geographic audience, then the language should be appropriate for that audience. If content is destined for the UK market, then write 'aeroplane' instead of 'airplane' and 'aluminium' rather than 'aluminum'. If you're writing for the US, be aware that 'pyjamas' is written as 'pajamas'; 'speciality' as 'specialty'. Know your spelling and make it consistent. A spell check might not catch subtle grammar mistakes, but set it to hunt for British English or US English spelling errors and it will do a great job of pointing out any that you've missed.

Poor apostrophe use
The apostrophe seems to confound some writers. So when proofreading, it's important to know when apostrophes should be used and when they shouldn't. Here's a quick run-down:

- Use apostrophes with contractions, including 'don't' (do not), 'won't' (will not), 'isn't' (is not), 'she's' (she is), 'he's' (he is), 'it's' (it is).
- Use apostrophes to show possession, even if the word ends in 's' - 'Next, it was David's turn', 'She tried on Ruth's jacket' or 'He had stolen his boss's car'.
- Use apostrophes to show plural possession - 'She

tried to find the Kumar's phone number' or 'Janet and John's house was in Devon'.

But DON'T use an apostrophe in words like 1980's, PC's or DVD's because it looks better. It should be 1980s, PCs and DVDs.

Proofreading test #3

Let's take a break for another test. Can you find the mistake(s) in this excerpt from a Second World War story. Again, this is a proofreading challenge, not a copy editing one, so be on the look out for spelling errors and incorrect punctuation. The answers follow...

— copy starts —

The battlefield was dark and unnervingly still. The men of the 2nd Battalion of the 13th Light Infantry, crouched in there trench. Some huddled impatiently around the cook-fires, while others sat diligently cleaning they're rifles. A few smoked spindly cigarettes or played cards with their fellow soldiers. But most had curled up, eyes shut, trying to catch up on two months of interrupted sleep.

"They're coming", whispered Private Hobbs.

"Where?" Beside Hobbs, Private Markwell shuffled forwards, peering over the edge of there trench and into the darkness. "I can't see anything. Are you sure?"

"There." Hobbs pointed to his left, towards a large crater in the churned black mud of No Man's Land. "There trying to stay low. But you can just see the moonlight shining on they're helmets. Wait a minute... There! Do you see them now?" Markwell nodded and slowly clicked a round into the chamber of his rifle.

"I wouldn't have seen them there otherwise," said Hobbs, raising his own rifle and squinting through the iron gun sight. "There tactic is damned clever. But it's not going

to work. Not this time. Alert the others..."
— copy ends —

Proofreading test #3 - Answers

This excerpt is primarily a test for the correct use of 'their', 'they're' and 'there'. They are homophones, words that sound the same but are spelt differently and have different meanings. There are several errors in the text, which are marked up in bold below.

— copy starts —
The battlefield was dark and unnervingly still. The men of the 2nd Battalion of the 13th Light Infantry, crouched in **there** trench. Some huddled impatiently around the cook-fires, while others sat diligently cleaning **they're** rifles. A few smoked spindly cigarettes or played cards with their fellow soldiers. But most had curled up, eyes shut, trying to catch up on two months of interrupted sleep.
"They're coming", whispered Private Hobbs.
"Where?" Beside Hobbs, Private Markwell shuffled forwards, peering over the edge of **there** trench and into the darkness. "I can't see anything. Are you sure?"
"There." Hobbs pointed to his left, towards a large crater in the churned black mud of No Man's Land. "**There** trying to stay low. But you can just see the moonlight shining on **they're** helmets. Wait a minute... There! Do you see them now?" Markwell nodded and slowly clicked a round into the chamber of his rifle.
"I wouldn't have seen them there otherwise," said Hobbs, raising his own rifle and squinting through the iron gun sight. "**There** tactic is damned clever. But it's not going to work. Not this time. Alert the others..."
— copy ends —

There: indicating a place, I.e. 'Over there'

51

They're: short for 'they are'
Their: indicating possession, I.e. 'their helmets'

Here's a corrected version of the text:

The battlefield was dark and unnervingly still. The men of the 2nd Battalion of the 13th Light Infantry, crouched in their trench. Some huddled impatiently around the cook-fires, while others sat diligently cleaning their rifles. A few smoked spindly cigarettes or played cards with their fellow soldiers. But most had curled up, eyes shut, trying to catch up on two months of interrupted sleep.

"They're coming", whispered Private Hobbs.

"Where?" Beside Hobbs, Private Markwell shuffled forwards, peering over the edge of their trench and into the darkness. "I can't see anything. Are you sure?"

"There." Hobbs pointed to his left, towards a large crater in the churned black mud of No Man's Land. "They're trying to stay low. But you can just see the moonlight shining on their helmets. Wait a minute... There! Do you see them now?" Markwell nodded and slowly clicked a round into the chamber of his rifle.

"I wouldn't have seen them there otherwise," said Hobbs, raising his own rifle and squinting through the iron gun sight. "Their tactic is damned clever. But it's not going to work. Not this time. Alert the others..."

Why we don't spot mistakes

I've already talked about ways to minimise mistakes when you write and by knowing some of the common mistakes people make, you can (a) try to avoid making them as a writer, and (b) aim to spot them more successfully when proofreading. Proofreading is the last line of defence. But even professional editors and proofreaders don't catch every error. Why?

Once again, it comes down to how we're wired. Our brains help us make sense of the world. They process all of the information that we see, hear, touch, taste and smell. In doing so, they often fill in information gaps for us based on previous experience. If you read a phrase that says 'He explained the flexibilty of the comercial process', you might spot that 'flexibility' and 'commercial' are spelt incorrectly. But it doesn't destroy the meaning of the sentence. Your brain can still understand what is being said.

You c*n st*ll unders***d t*is

The theory of 'predictive coding' maintains that the brain doesn't simply process sensory information as it arrives. Speaking to *PhysOrg.com*, Dr Lars Muckli, from Glasgow University's Institute of Neuroscience and Psychology explained that "we are continuously anticipating what we will see, hear or feel next. If parts of an image are obstructed we still have precise expectation of what the whole object will look like."

This is why we can still understand a sentence even if some of the words that appear in that sent**ce have m*ssing le**ers. Or they hve wrds taht r miss spelt and contayn lotz of eroars. Take a look at this mangled text excerpt that was circulated on the Internet a few years ago:

"Aoccdrnig to a rscheearch at Cmabrigde Uinervtisy, it deosn't mttaer in waht oredr the ltteers in a wrod are, the olny iprmoetnt tihng is taht the frist and lsat ltteer be at the rghit pclae. The rset can be a toatl mses and you can sitll raed it wouthit a porbelm. Tihs is bcuseae the huamn mnid deos not raed ervey lteter by istlef, but the wrod as a wlohe."

You should be able to decipher it surprisingly quickly, almost as if the spelling errors aren't there. It should read:

"According to a researcher at Cambridge University, it

doesn't matter in what order the letters in a word are, the only important thing is that the first and last letter be at the right place. The rest can be a total mess and you can still read it without a problem. This is because the human mind does not read every letter by itself but the word as a whole."

Ignore the content of the previous text - Cambridge University didn't do any such research. At least not according to Matt Davis, who works at Cambridge University's Cognition and Brain Sciences Unit (CBSU).

But there's still a key lesson here, which is that most of us do not read every letter individually. We read words as a whole. We also expect words to be a certain shape. This makes it easier for us to spot a spelling error like 'taht', because it defies the recognisable shape of the correct word, 'that'. But it's much harder to spot an error such as 'heirarchy', where two similar letters are transposed. The correct spelling is 'hierarchy'. As you can see, the shape of the two words is the same.

Those pesky flying monkeys

Davis, who studies how the brain processes spoken and written language, has suggested that we can process the jumbled text quickly because "transpositions of adjacent letters (e.g. 'porbelm' for 'problem') are easier to read than more distant transpositions (e.g. 'pborlem')." He goes onto explain that, "we know from research in which people read words presented very briefly on a computer screen that the exterior letters of words are easier to detect than middle letters."

Transposed letters are like flying monkeys to the proofreader's Dorothy. Annoying and difficult to catch. It helps explain why we might not notice 'unweildy' when it should be 'unwieldy' or that 'flourescent' is catastrophically incorrect and should be 'fluorescent'. Ultimately, poor spelling isn't a barrier to comprehension and the secret to good proofreading is to try and read the words without absorbing context and meaning. Easy to say, harder to do in practice.

The closer you are to the words on the page, the harder it becomes to completely disconnect from them. This is why it's difficult to proofread something that you've written. Your familiarity with the content can subconsciously encourage you to skip over words and phrases. In your head, you might see words and phrases as correct when they are anything but. You read what you think is on the page, not always what is actually on the page. Here's a quick experiment... Try counting the number of 'F's in the text that follows:

FINISHED FILES ARE THE RE
SULT OF YEARS OF SCIENTI
FIC STUDY COMBINED WITH
THE EXPERIENCE OF YEARS.

How many did you see? If you saw three, you're wrong. Four? That's wrong too. There are six 'F's in this example, but many people only see the 'F's in 'FINISHED', 'FILES' and, because of the way the text is laid out, the 'F' in 'SCIENTIFIC'. But there are another three 'F's in the three 'OF's. Here's another one...

I
LOVE
PARIS IN THE
THE SPRINGTIME

Did you spot the double word? If you didn't, read it again and it becomes obvious. By processing the meaning of the words, rather than the words in isolation, it's possible to miss the simplest of spelling/formatting errors.

Don't trust your spell check

One of the other reasons that we don't spot mistakes is that we don't look for them properly. Word processors have made writing easier. But they've also made writers lazier. Spelling and grammar is often an afterthought in a world that demands the ceaseless production of good content. Consequently, it's tempting to leave error-hunting to a spell checker. It's better than nothing. But proofreading isn't as simple as a spell check, and running a spell check shouldn't be a replacement for spending some time re-reading text before you print or publish it.

Because your spell check will lie to you. It will tell you that everything you've written is fine. Don't worry. Breathe easy. It's got you covered. But while context-sensitive spell check algorithms will catch a lot of basic mistakes, they are far from perfect. A spell check won't, for example, pick up on some correctly-spelt words used incorrectly in a sentence. It won't recognise the correct spellings of most people and places. Nor can it query facts, dates or events. Truth be told, a word processor isn't actually that good at spotting clumsy grammar.

Don't get me wrong. A spell check is a useful tool as part of the proofreading process. But good text-checking requires a human eye. A proofreader's eye. Preferably two. You want proof? Here's how clever the average spell check is... Take a look at the text excerpt that follows and see how many mistakes you can spot.

— *copy starts* —
Simone pointed his finger the boy and smiled wicked smile. "So you've peddled all night to get here?' He said. "Impressive. We've not too far from border here. You may also see also Scotland if you climb up to top of that hill over there too."

"Thanks Simon," replied *th*e boy.

"One more thing... I cut my knee earlier and hadn't brought a 1st aid kid along. To be honest, my memory hasn't been goof over the past few years as it used to be. Do you have one that I could burrow?"

— copy ends —

There are a total of 19 deliberate mistakes in this short passage and Microsoft Word 2010 doesn't find any of them. The spell checker baked into Google Drive finds two, as does Ginger Software's free online spell check (but not the same two). Here's the text excerpt again, with the errors highlighted in bold.

Simone pointed **his** finger **the boy** and smiled **wicked** smile. "So you've **peddled** all night to get **here?'** **He said**. "Impressive. **We've** not too far **from border** here. You **may** also see **also** Scotland if you climb up **to top** of that hill over there **too**."

"Thanks **Simon**," replied *th*e boy.

"One more thing... I cut my knee earlier and **hadn't** brought a **1st** aid **kid** along. To be honest, my memory hasn't **been goof** over the past few years as it used to be. Do you have one that I could **burrow**?"

his: As the person pointing is called Simone, this should be 'her finger'

the boy: 'at the boy'

wicked: there's a missing 'a' - 'smiled a wicked smile'

peddled: 'pedalled'

here?': note the single quote mark/apostrophe that ends this speech. It should be a double quote.

He said: Again, the person speaking is called Simone and is female, therefore it should read 'She said.'

We've: Should be 'We're' - 'We're not too far...'

from border: missing 'the' - 'from the border'

may: 'can'

also: there are two 'also's in quick succession. We only need one.

to top: 'to the top'

too: The sentence doesn't need 'too' when it already has 'also'

Simon: We've already identified that the character is called Simone

the: See the italics applied to the 't' and 'h' of 'the'? They shouldn't be there.

hadn't: 'haven't'

1st: 'first'

kid: 'kit'

been goof: 'been as good'

burrow: This should be 'borrow'. No digging involved.

The text here passed online spell checkers JSpell and spellcheck.net without raising any flags. It also skipped through Ginger Software's free online tool, which only spotted 'a wicked smile' and changed 'peddled' to the equally incorrect 'paddled'. Google Drive picked up the fact that it should have been first aid 'kit' not 'kid'. It also flagged 'goof'. Still trust a spell check? No, neither do I.

4. How many proofreaders...

Q. How many proofreaders does it take to change a light bulb?

A. None. 'A light bulb' is grammatically correct.

Improve your proofreading and copy editing

If we assume that, despite our best efforts, some mistakes are always going to slip through when we create content, then the last line of defence is always a rigorous copy check. I tend to split this into three stages - first, a deep copy edit, followed by a sense check (to make sure that the copy edit hasn't created any new errors), and lastly a thorough proofread, examining every word.

In this chapter, we'll look at each of these stages in detail, revealing some key copy editing tips and the different ways that you can proofread quickly and successfully. We'll also hear from professional copy editors and proofreaders to see how they approach the process of copy checking. And if you're wondering whether proofreading software is worth using, we'll look at those options too.

Plus we'll explore ways of increasing your concentration, so that it's easier to spot even the trickiest of grammatical goofs. The end result is that you'll have the tools to help you spot any lingering mistakes in your content before you publish it. But before we get to all this, I'm going to add a fourth stage into the process. It slots in right at the beginning and is especially important if you plan to edit and proofread your own work. It's simply this...

Get some distance

If you can't get somebody else to check your work (and you aren't pressured by a deadline that's hurtling towards you like a runaway express train), don't start with a copy edit just yet. Try leaving some time between writing and checking. Whether you've just finished putting together a blog post, brochure, report, memo or PowerPoint presentation, try walking away from the text for a few hours. If you're able to, sleep on it.

When you've spent time absorbed in a writing task, it's good to step away from it, so that the familiarity you have with the structure of the words and phrases can begin to fade. You can accelerate this process by writing something else, reading a book or watching TV. Remember how the human brain can't effectively process more than two tasks at once? Disconnect with your content by connecting with something different.

By getting some distance between you and your work, you can approach it later with a freshened eye. If you're a writer/publisher and check your own work, it's the next best thing to having a proofreader who has no connection to what they're reading. Try it. You might return to your work and be surprised that it reads better than you remember. Happy days. Or you might spot 17 errors right off the bat and realise that your content doesn't live up to the idea in your head. Whatever happens, you'll get a different perspective on your content before you dive into the copy edit.

Proofreading test #4

Speaking of familiarity, take a look at the text that follows.

I'll test you on it later in the book.

— copy starts —

Editing isn't necessarily about rewriting. It's about tightening text, firming up ideas and polishing presentation. Take out repetitive words where possible and be on the lookout for tense-switching. Don't forget to check other elements beyond the main copy, such as captions, page numbers, pull-out quotes, headlines and subheadings. Check contractions too, such as 'won't' and 'can't'. Ask whether they are appropriate for your content. More formal documents will usually feature 'cannot' rather than 'can't'.

— copy ends —

Copy editing tips

"When subbing, the focus is on the detail - every letter counts - not just the overall sense. Being able to step into a different mind set is essential. Everyone subs differently but there are some basics. Make sure you have read the copy all the way through before you change anything to make sure you understand the whole text. Once you have finished editing, read it all the way through again to make sure it still makes sense. No one is infallible and even the best sub-eds make mistakes. The secret to getting it right is being confident about what you do know and looking up what you don't." - *Holly Bowman, Website Manager for www.t3.com, www.techradar.com and www.gizmodo.co.uk*

Copy editing somebody else's work

Most of the tips that follow are applicable whether you're editing your own work or someone else's. The words will be sitting there in front of you, seemingly perfect. So what happens next? A good copy edit takes rough-edged, raw copy and bangs it into a more pleasing shape. It smooths over first draft imperfections and polishes content until it shines.

It's about developing a system. A process. A single read-through won't cut it. A good process will usually involve multiple read-throughs and several edits. Your first read-through should be to get a feel for the content and the ideas/themes it is trying to convey, whether it flows and whether anything is unclear, incorrect or potentially confusing.

The first edit will obviously take the longest. It tackles the deepest flaws and makes the biggest changes. If you're editing an article, brochure, newsletter or something similar, this is where you'll typically cut and add info, trim sentences and slice unsightly chunks of text into smaller, more digestible paragraphs. This is also where you'll potentially optimise the text so it's easier to read, adding subheadings, writing (or rewriting) headlines if required, and adding relevant picture captions. Of course, this will depend on where the content will eventually be published. A website article should have short and snappy paragraphs. The text in an instruction manual or white paper will generally be denser and have fewer formatting frills.

Your first read-through

You might be tempted to start editing the text on your first read-through. Or to run a spell check. Don't do either. Try to avoid knee-jerk editing the words in a sentence without having read the full paragraph and absorbing the context. Similarly, it's a good idea to reserve judgements about the text until you've read the whole thing. You can't successfully edit something without first understanding it. A hands-off read-through will help you mentally flag problem areas that you'll fix in the subsequent edit.

Be sure to keep a copy of the unedited text too, just in

case you make changes and then want to revert back to the original.

Your second read-through/first edit

Whatever content you're editing - an article, blog post, brochure text, website text, newsletter, thesis, book or essay - there are some key questions to ask as you read through the copy for the first time. Questions like...

Is it what you want? If you haven't written the content that you're about to edit, consider whether it fulfils the brief or commission for the work. There's little point spending time editing something that doesn't fulfil your publishing requirements. If there are only a few omissions, and you have sufficient knowledge of the subject matter, then you might be able to add in any missing information. Otherwise, fling the copy back at the original writer and get them to resubmit another version.

Does everything make sense? Are the ideas being expressed clearly? Is there anything that's been missed out? Are there any questions that the content leaves unanswered for the reader? If you didn't write the copy that you're editing then you're better equipped to tackle these questions. If you're confused about something, there's a good chance that a reader will feel the same way. You might also see spelling errors as you start to edit, so fix them as you go. Don't worry about spotting everything. You'll pick up any lingering errors in the third read-through.

Does the copy flow? Do you need to edit any long sentences to make them more concise? Or break up chunky paragraphs? Think: is there a simpler way to say things? A shorter way? A better way? (Remember that the answer can be 'no'...) Good copy editing shouldn't involve drastic rewrites. Also be on the lookout for sentences that breathlessly run and run, linked with commas and too many 'and's, 'but's, 'yet's, 'because's and 'however's. Fix them.

Does the copy get straight to the point? Or does it dally? Professional production editors/copy editors often suggest throwing away the first line or even the first paragraph of a long article as a matter of course. It's often padding - writers sometimes delay getting to the point quickly. Consider cutting from the front to see whether it improves the content and gives it a punchier opening. If it doesn't, just put the words back. No harm done.

If the content is long, is it too long? How well does it hold your attention? Are you bored? If you are, there's a good chance that the reader will be too. Look for passages that repeat what's already been said and repeat what's already been said... Be vigilant. Sentences might roll out the same information in a different way. If you're working in print, do you need to cut the copy back to fit a specific word count or page length? What can you safely chop out without losing key information or damaging the flow? Finally, if the copy is one long chunk of text, would it benefit from the addition of meaningful subheadings to keep the reader's attention as they progress from introduction to conclusion?

Is the content too short? Will the reader feel cheated by the content because it doesn't include enough information? You can either add extra information yourself, or return the copy to the original writer.

Are the facts correct? Double check every fact you see, even if you think there's nothing wrong with them. Query all numbers, dates, maps, calculations, names, places, products, measurements and directions. At first glance, there doesn't appear to be anything wrong with this sentence: 'Venice is only the start of your journey... Head east, past Padua, and you reach the fair city of Verona, where Shakespeare's Romeo and Juliet became star-crossed lovers.' But you actually head 'west', past Padua...

Is anything offensive or libellous? When I joined my

first publishing company as a young writer, the first course they packed me off on was about libel. It's important to know what can get you into trouble, whether you're writing, editing and proofreading your own content or editing/proofreading somebody else's work.

Libel is defined as: "to publish in print (including pictures), writing or broadcast through radio, television or film, an untruth about another which will do harm to that person or his/her reputation, by tending to bring the target into ridicule, hatred, scorn or contempt of others. Libel is the written or broadcast form of defamation, distinguished from slander which is oral defamation."

Some thoughts on rewriting

Editing isn't necessarily about rewriting. It's about tightening text, firming up ideas and polishing presentation. Take out repetitive words where possible. Be on the look out for tense-switching. Be sure to check other elements beyond the main copy, such as captions, page numbers, pull-out quotes, headlines and subheadings. Check contractions too, such as 'won't' and 'can't'. Ask whether they are appropriate for your content? More formal documents will usually feature 'cannot' rather than 'can't'.

George Orwell's six rules of writing can prove to be a handy guide for copy editors and proofreaders, who can apply them when writers forget. They are:

1. "Never use a metaphor, simile, or other figure of speech that you are used to seeing in print" - If you see a cliche or an overused word/phrase, slice it out or substitute it for something less common.

2. "Never use a long word where a short one will do" - You might think that fancy words will impress your readers... They won't if they can't understand them. Write/edit using language that is appropriate for your

intended audience and favour simple words over complex ones.

3. "If it is possible to cut a word out, always cut it out" - In other words, don't let sentences ramble. Try to eliminate unnecessary adjectives and wishy-washy qualifier words, such as 'very', 'fairly', 'rather', 'probably', 'somewhat' and 'almost'.

4. "Never use the passive where you can use the active" - Delete a sentence that says - 'the hero was knocked down by the evil henchman', and replace it with a more active version - 'the henchman knocked down the hero'.

5. "Never use a foreign phrase, a scientific word or a jargon word if you can think of an everyday English equivalent" - Again, the language you use should be appropriate for your intended audience. If the content is aimed at a knowledgeable readership, then they'll typically understand niche jargon and acronyms. But a more general or beginner-type audience might not get the references and you risk alienating them.

6. "Break any of these rules sooner than say anything outright barbarous" - Bend or break these rules if you need to. Don't let language be a barrier to information or entertainment.

Copy editing your own work

How does all this change if you've written the content yourself? You probably won't ask yourself all of the same questions. And if you do, you might not be as rigorous in asking them. But the aim is the same: to take the first draft of what you've written and to improve it, trimming, clarifying and double-checking every word.

The depth of your self-edit will depend on what sort of writer you are. Do you write and rewrite, polishing each sentence before moving onto the next one? Or do you try to write as fast as possible, getting everything down onto the page as fast as you can, knowing that you'll edit it later?

Everything that I've just talked about applies here, even the 'is it what you want?' question. You might be thinking: 'of course the copy is what I want. I wrote it!' But don't be precious about your words. Consider whether what you've written is fulfilling the reason that you've written it. Does it deliver on what the headline promises? Have you answered all of a reader's potential questions? Is the content useful? It's easy to miss small details that don't matter much to you, but are vital for readers.

Go through the list of questions: does your content get straight to the point? Is it too long? Are the facts correct? Have you avoided saying anything libellous? When checking your own work, it can be difficult to ask yourself whether it 'makes sense' and whether it 'flows'. Your initial answer will always be 'yes'. But try a tactic from the proofreader's toolbox. Read your content out loud. If you stumble over the words or notice that you've missed something out, then the flow isn't as smooth as it could be. Similarly, if you run out of breath before you reach some form of punctuation in a sentence, then your copy isn't as perfect as you might have hoped.

When self-editing, resist the temptation to make changes just for the sake of making changes. The more you rewrite or try new words out to see if they're better, the greater the chance that you'll make new errors. Small errors in key places can have huge consequences. Imagine missing a phone number or contact email address off a brochure when it's too late to recall it from the printers. Or forgetting to put the correct barcode/price on a magazine cover and having to pay someone to individually sticker 30,000 copies. Details matter.

There's a lot to remember here. Check out the copy editing checklist in the Appendix.

The third and fourth read-throughs

Post edit, you need a third read-through to hunt for any lingering mechanical errors that you haven't already spotted - spelling, punctuation, consistency and grammar. This moves us into proofreading territory...

Proofreading tips

"Perhaps strangely, my first read-through looks for typos and punctuation errors, while a second scan accesses that part of my brain that wants to understand what's being said. So, paragraph structure and story comprehension play second fiddle to an errant colon or Oxford comma. I generally read each section of two or three paragraphs twice, regardless of deadlines. If I'm proofing for somebody else and it's required that I leave marks in the margins, I don't use proofreading symbols." - *Shaun Weston, Managing Editor Digital, FoodBev Media Ltd*

When proofreading content, you're either approaching it cold (you've never seen it before) or you're settling in to look for errors after an edit. The content might be something you've written or something that's been created by a colleague or an external contributor. Whatever the situation, the proofreading tips here all apply. The aim is same - to scrape away spelling, punctuation and grammar errors to leave smooth and polished content behind.

Don't rush in. If you've written the content you're about to proofread, I've already suggested that you try to get some distance from it before you start to edit. The same advice applies when it comes to a proofreading session. Build in some extra time to forget what you've just edited. Of course, you can ignore this advice if you're proofreading the content and have no previous connection with it. If that's the case, you'll obviously be approaching it with fresh eyes and no bias.

Get the right tools for the job. When I first started out
in publishing, every copy editor, sub-editor and production
editor had the following within easy reach - a hardback
copy of the Oxford English Dictionary, Roget's Thesaurus,
a copy of their magazine's style guide, a ruler, a cup of tea,
plus an armoury of red pens for highlighting mistakes and
scribbling amendments on printed pages.

These days, you can replace the books with links to
dictionary.reference.com and thesaurus.reference.com. The
classic red pens are no longer an essential tool either - a lot
of proofreading is now done onscreen to save time and
paper. As for the ruler... this was often useful to block out
lines below the one being proofed. It's a tactic that works
well on paper, but not so well on a computer screen.

Know what to look for. Did you notice that the last
paragraph mentioned a 'style guide'? You should have one.
Find out why later in this chapter.

Minimise distractions. Proofreading requires
concentration and it's all too easy to get distracted. Block
out some time to work through the text, ignoring your
phone, email, Twitter, Facebook and, if you work in an
office, other people. Don't let anything shift your focus
away from the words on the page or the screen in front of
you. Make sure your seat is comfortable, that you have a
drink nearby if you need it, that you have enough light and
enough time to do a thorough job.

Forget proofreading symbols. Unless you want to
become a proofreader for a book publisher, you won't need
to learn proofreading symbols. Many of us now work with
websites, blogs, ebooks and desktop publishing software
and these textual and marginal symbols have become all
but redundant. They can still be useful if you regularly print
out content for checking. Or when the person doing the
proofreading isn't the person that makes the corrections. In
this case, a common set of symbols enables changes to be

communicated without any confusion. If you'd like to see the British Standard BS 5261 proofreading marks, you can find them linked in the Appendix.

Read slowly. The average adult reading speed is between 200 and 250 words per minute, which means that most people can digest a 500 word article in around two minutes. A good proofreader will generally read much slower than this, lingering a little longer on each word. So rather than reading a sentence at speed, like this. It's... Better... To... Read... A... Sentence... Much... Slower... Like... This. Reading this way enables you to concentrate on the spelling of each word rather than the meaning of the sentence.

Different ways to proofread

"My proofreading has changed since I moved from the magazine trade to working primarily with online media. Very close and careful reading of text is something that has persisted during the transition. Multiple read-throughs are key, as the first time you tend to focus on the details - sentences making sense grammatically, punctuation, word repetition, spelling of company names and acronyms. The next read-through will bring things up a level to the flow of a piece of work. Further read-throughs will allow you to focus on the overall sense of the whole article." - *Dr James Morris, Web Media Producer and Lecturer*

There's no right way to proofread. Besides, what works for one proofreader might not be as effective for another. Try the proofreading methods below to see which one you find most effective. Many of them simply try to reduce your familiarity with the text and its meaning so you can concentrate on checking the grammar, spelling and formatting.

Print the content out. This old-school method still

works because it enables you to get up close and personal with the text. Print out your article and go through it by tapping each word with the proofreader's weapon of choice – a red biro. Tapping each word will slow down your reading speed and encourage you to focus on whether each word is spelt correctly. It's a technique that can also work onscreen. Simply replace the pen with the mouse cursor - move it over each word as you read to allow your brain more time to process what you're seeing. If you're proofreading on a tablet, touch each word with a finger or stylus.

I'm a fan of printing out large projects. But I prefer to work digitally these days. A good compromise that works for me is to output a writing draft as a PDF, then import it into a PDF editor app on the iPad. I use GoodNotes, which enables me to scribble notes onscreen in the same way that I'd write corrections on a physical proof.

Split the check. This method involves going through the text multiple times, once to search for spelling mistakes, a second time to hunt for punctuation problems, and a third pass to check for any grammatical goofs. By doing so, you're not on alert for every type of error. You can focus on a particular type, before moving onto the next one.

Reformat the content. By changing the appearance of text you're working with, you can reduce the familiarity of the layout. When you work with a piece of text for any length of time, the structure of it becomes fixed in your mind and it gets harder to spot errors. By increasing, reducing or changing the font, viewing the content on a different device, or in a different software package, you can reformat the content anew, changing the position of line breaks and altering paragraph sizes. This reformatting forces you to read the text in a different way, giving you another opportunity to root out errors that you might have missed.

Read the content backwards. This is another useful way of reducing your familiarity with the text so you can concentrate on the structure of the words and sentences. You can either read every sentence backwards (good for focusing on spelling) or read each sentence forwards, but in reverse order. This means tackling the last sentence of a paragraph first, followed by the second-to-last sentence, and so on. This approach still disrupts the flow of the paragraph but enables you to check for spelling, punctuation and grammar.

Read the content out loud. Again, this is an attempt to strip away any familiarity you have with the layout of the text. By reading your article aloud, you'll notice sentences that are too long (because you can't say them without pausing for breath). You'll stumble over incorrect words and typos, spot inconsistencies, and detect when the rhythm or pacing of a paragraph just isn't right. I know authors who spend an entire day reading their work in progress novels out loud because it helps them spot overlong sentences, poor punctuation and word repetition.

What to look for when proofreading

"I check copy against the commission first. Once I know I've got everything and it's the right word count, I read it through giving it a good sub as I go. This involves checking all facts the first time, plus spellings of names/companies etc. Then I'll go back and scan it again onscreen to check that I've got everything. If it's a big feature I'll print it off and read through the paper copy before sending it over to art... I'll then read it again once it's been laid out. But the copy should be perfect by then, so it's more of a final check..." - *Julia Sagar, Production Editor, Computer Arts magazine*

Proofreading is the last line of quality control. This isn't the time to be rewriting sentences or adding in new information. It's an error-hunt, plain and simple. As such, it requires a slightly different mindset and a great deal of concentration. You can't rely on a word processor to proofread for you. So start by assuming that everything is wrong and ask yourself these questions as you check spelling, punctuation, grammar and formatting...

Is the spelling accurate? There's no shame in looking up words that you're not sure about, even easy ones. There are times when even the best writers can't spell the simplest words. Yesterday, for example, I struggled to spell the word 'entirety'. It doesn't have two 'i's ('entirity') and I know full well that it doesn't have two 'i's. But my mind went strangely blank and I couldn't think of any other way to write it. Traditional proofreaders and copy editors often have a giant dictionary within easy reach. But you can just as easily use dictionary.reference.com or just type words that you're not sure about into a Google search. You'll get an answer in seconds.

Is the spelling consistent? We've seen that you can't entirely trust a spell check, especially when problem words aren't part of a word processor's internal dictionary. So if you encounter names that are spelt differently throughout an article, never assume that the first spelling you see is the correct one. Or that the most used spelling is correct one. Similarly, check that acronyms are correct throughout. Don't skip past the phrase 'Los Angeles Police Department' but forget to check that it says 'LAPD' and not 'LADP' later.

Have I missed any homophones? Check for words that sound the same but are spelt differently and have different meanings, such as: 'their', 'there' and 'they're'; 'compleat' and 'complete'; 'compliment' and 'complement'.

Does it make sense? We asked this question during the copy edit, but it's worth asking again. Some errors might not be immediately apparent. There might be mismatched subjects and verbs. So if you see 'there's lots of animals in this park', it should be 'there are lots of animals in this park'. You might also encounter tense-switching between past and present. 'I look up and who did I see?' is wrong. 'I looked up and who did I see?' is correct.

Does anything sound ridiculous? Consider word choice. Be on the look-out for outbreaks of acute 'Thesaurusitis'. This is a debilitating condition that encourages writers to choose 'splendorous' when they should be using 'superb', or 'hardihood' instead of 'confidence'. A simple approach to language is best, but you don't want to eradicate the writer's voice by editing it out completely. Find a good balance.

Are any words missing? Watch out for AWOL words in the content. We've already seen that a sentence like 'Simone pointed his finger the boy and smiled wicked smile' can slip by a word processor spell check unchallenged, even though it's missing an 'at' and an 'a'. Focus on checking the little words that are easily missed, including 'the', 'in', 'on', 'up', 'it' and 'to'.

Are any sentences missing? Check for key elements that haven't been written, such as headlines, subheadings, table titles, captions and footnotes. Check anything that is not part of the main copy. Then check for those elements that have been written, but might have been written incorrectly. Remember 'Type some s**t in here please'? You don't want to make that mistake.

Are text references correct? If you see the words 'see page 56', check that (a) there actually is a 'page 56' and (b) that the text references some information on that page. If you're working on a website, it's also worth testing links and email addresses to make sure that they work.

Is the style consistent? A style guide can help you with this. See the 'Style Guide' section later in this chapter.

Is the punctuation correct? There are lots of things to watch out for. Too many commas. Not enough commas. A complete absence of commas. Commas where semi-colons should be (and vice-versa). Don't add question marks to the end of sentences that actually aren't questions. Be sure to check apostrophes, primarily 'its' and 'it's' ('it is'). 'DVD's' as a plural is wrong, 'DVDs' is right. Check full-stops. Double-check the correct deployment of quotation marks (don't use them for "emphasis"), and know that using more than one exclamation mark at the end of a sentence will get you sent to the naughty step.

Is the formatting clean? Beyond spelling and grammar errors, how does the content look? Are the fonts correct? Is the text the right size? Does it all line up neatly? Are there any double spaces between words or after full stops? If there's a top 10 list, are there 10 things in that list? Are they numbered correctly? Speaking of numbers, if you're working on a print project, have you checked that the pages are numbered correctly?

Whether you're proofreading an article, a report, a thesis or a full-length book, a good proofreading session will let no word go unchecked. As before, always re-read a sentence in its entirety if you've changed any words within it. You could unknowingly be creating new errors. Finally, run a spell check. With the edit complete and a proofread in the bag, now is a perfect time to let a spell check have its algorithmic way with the content. If you find any errors, fix them and then give the whole thing another read-through just to be sure.

What good is a style guide?

A style guide is essentially a blueprint of editorial dos and don'ts that helps to ensure uniformity of tone, style, formatting and spelling in everything that you publish under a particular brand. This might include the way that you write dates, use acronyms, italicise titles, even how headlines are written and what captions should be about. It might specify whether the tone is conversational, independent, opinionated or neutral, and whether you talk to the reader with 'you' or remain more detached and anonymous.

Using a style guide can help you write, edit and proofread consistently and eliminate confusion for your readers. For example, you run the risk of looking amateurish if you spell words differently in the same piece of content - I.e. 'email' as 'e-mail' and then as 'e mail' (twice) before using 'e-mail' again. Ditto formatting. How did you emphasise a word in the last bit of content you wrote or edited? Did you use bold? Italics? Was it CAPS? With a style guide, you simply specify your preferred spelling or formatting and stick to it.

Having a style guide makes the copy editing and proofreading processes easier as you have a ready-made list of guidelines, problem words and examples to check against. Not only that, but a style guide can also include some information about readership - who is the publication aimed at, the age range, how much knowledge of the brand/subject they have, and so on.

Style guides are used by newspapers, magazines and websites, where maintaining a professional feel is just as important as allowing individual editorial voices to shine through. They lay down the content rules when multiple writers, editors or proofreaders work on a brand. The combination of a good brief and a decent style guide can help you get the content you need, correctly formatted, so you don't have to spend extra time editing it.

That's not to say a style guide isn't useful for solo writer/publishers like bloggers or small business owners who create their own marketing materials. It takes a bit of effort to set up a style guide. But the longer-term benefits, plus the way that it aids copy editing and proofreading, outweigh the short-term work.

But what should a style guide contain? According to *The Guardian Style Guide*, written and edited by David

Marsh for *The Guardian* newspaper in the UK, a style guide "can be a subtle business. Many entries emphasise distinctions between words often misused or confused: doner, kebab; donor, gives money (did someone resist the temptation to say "donor, kidney"?); hyperthermia, hot; hypothermia, cold; disinterested, free from bias or objective; uninterested, not taking an interest; hangar for aircraft, hanger for clothes. Grammar is defined, while saving us all the shame of pointing out that it occasionally appears as grammer."

A style guide should include:

- What the tone and feel of the copy should be, with examples. I.e. "the tone is chatty and irreverent... like a best friend with a bit more knowledge than you".
- A preferred spelling and grammar list: company names, trademarks, people ('J.K Rowling' or 'JK Rowling'?), places, measurements, commonly used words/phrases and their preferred spellings. I.e. is it 'World War II' or 'World War 2'?
- How you write dates - 13 July, July 13, July 13th, 13th July etc.
- How you write numbers - are measurements 2cm or 2 cm? Do you write one to nine, 10-99,999? Is it 15% or 15 per cent?
- A list of words you're NOT allowed to use, such as this wishy-washy trio: 'quite', 'pretty' and 'reasonably'
- Whether you're using American or British spelling (for English speakers)
- Whether you're formal or informal - do you use contractions such as 'don't' instead of 'do not'?
- How much personality you project: do you use 'I' or 'we'?

- Whether you can swear
- When you use certain fonts or text sizes - i.e. media names should always be italicised, the first paragraph is always in bold, and so on
- When subheads should be used and whether they have a full stop
- When you should deploy CAPITAL LETTERS
- How, when and where you should add web links
- Caption styles – do your captions have full stops on the end or not?
- Style of humour
- When to hyphenate (and when not to)
- How long a typical article should be
- Key information that appears in certain places and its order, i.e a spec box or info box
- Editorial traps that writers often fall into - I.e. companies and organisations are singular - 'the BBC is', not 'the BBC are'

A word of warning: don't get carried away documenting every teeny-tiny stylistic element. Big style guides can become confusing and unwieldy. Keep things simple and logical. There's a style guide template in the Appendix to get you started.

Improve your concentration

So far we've discussed why we make mistakes, what sort of mistakes we make, and why we don't always spot them. We've also looked at tips and tactics for copy editing and proofreading content. But having the skills and knowledge to spot errors in content is one thing. Maintaining the concentration required to methodically check every word and every comma is quite another.

Proofreading is an essential part of the publishing

process. Doing a thorough job usually involves reading, re-reading and re-re-reading the same words, hunting for mistakes that might not even be there. It can be difficult to focus and remain alert during each copy-checking pass. The potential for distraction increases with every read-through and if your focus is jolted, there's an increased chance that you will (a) miss a mistake or (b) create a new error when editing.

Do you often find your concentration starting to wander? If you do, you're not alone. Attention spans for all types of media seem to have shortened dramatically. We expect a book to grab us in the first few pages, a film to keep us hooked from the opening sequence. We skip and scan web pages if the text is too dense or if an article doesn't immediately satisfy our reason for clicking through to it.

Self-sabotage

As the number of distractions in our lives has increased, our ability to concentrate on a single task for a decent period of time has diminished. Sometimes, the hardest part of doing a task is making a start on it. We'll often do anything to avoid something that we're not fully committed to, such as making another cup of tea when you've only just finished one or promoting another task that is actually less important. Saying to yourself 'I'll just quickly do this task before I start...' is another form of self-sabotage. There's usually nothing quick about checking your email, Facebook, Twitter or one of your favourite websites.

When you have started a task like proofreading, it's often difficult to maintain momentum. You invite distraction, whether you admit it or not, whether you want to or not. As a human being, you can't help yourself. To retain your focus, you can try giving yourself an incentive or promising yourself a reward for finishing the task.

Bribery can work wonders. But if you want to increase your concentration, you need to identify and eliminate potential distractions.

So turn that mobile phone off. Minimise the Internet. Ignore email. Put headphones on. Have all the tools you need to hand - pens, paper, dictionaries, food and drink. Tell people you're going to be busy. If you can reduce background noise, all the better.

It's also important to make yourself comfortable, because your environment can have a negative impact on your productivity. Cornell University professor Alan Hedge asserted in a 2004 study that productivity takes a noticeable dip when your workspace is too hot or too cold, too noisy, too dim or too bright, or if you have a lack of privacy.

What's interesting here is the idea that the temperature of your chosen workspace can have a dramatic effect on your concentration and productivity. *Fast Company* magazine summed up the Cornell study, which fiddled with the office temperature in a Florida insurance company and documented the results. In an article entitled 'Want More Productive Workers? Adjust Your Thermostat', Ron Friedman wrote: "When temperatures were low (68 degrees, to be precise), employees committed 44% more errors and were less than half as productive as when temperatures were warm (a cozy 77 degrees)."

How does a cold office affect concentration? According to the same *Fast Company* article: "When our body's temperature drops, we expend energy keeping ourselves warm, making less energy available for concentration, inspiration, and insight."

Ideally, work somewhere quiet and warm, somewhere bland and uninteresting. Consider that too much artificial light can make you more prone to distraction as the day goes on. To combat this, try working in shorter bursts, splitting large pieces of content into smaller chunks. This enables you to take regular breaks to rest your eyes. It also encourages you to step away from your computer and recharge your batteries by going outside for some fresh air and natural daylight.

It's also important not to multitask when proofreading. If you have 100% of your attention to devote to tasks, splitting this between two tasks (50/50 or 75/25) won't enable you to be effective at either of them. Not only that, but it will probably take you longer to complete two tasks if you work on them simultaneously, rather than sequentially.

This is why it can be helpful to split the copy-checking process down into a number of separate passes. Try looking for all of the spelling errors first, then the punctuation errors, then the grammar and formatting mistakes. Or note down all of the mistakes you see on an initial pass, then go back through the copy to make changes. Create your own routine or process and stick to it. The structure this gives you can help you focus on the job in hand.

If you lose your concentration at any point, think about the consequences of doing a sloppy job. Why are you copy editing and proofreading? You're eliminating errors, eradicating spelling mistakes and rooting out rotten formatting. If an error gets through, it will be your fault. It will reflect badly on you and the brand that you represent. Translate this responsibility into doing a thorough check. In the ongoing war against typos, a proofreader is the last line of defence.

Let's recap. Here are seven tips to help you improve your concentration and become a better copy-checker.

1. Give yourself an incentive to finish
2. Eliminate distractions
3. Work somewhere quiet
4. Make yourself comfortable
5. Work in short bursts and take regular breaks
6. Don't multitask
7. Consider the consequences of doing a bad job

Finally, take your time. Don't rush through a copy editing or proofreading session, unless someone is screaming at you for copy...

Proofreading test #4, part two

Here's the same text that I showed you earlier. By reading it through again, you're not just building up a familiarity with the words and sentences, but with where the words appear and the overall shape of the content. It will be interesting to see whether you can spot the errors when they are added later.

— copy starts —
Editing isn't necessarily about rewriting. It's about tightening text, firming up ideas and polishing presentation. Take out repetitive words where possible and be on the lookout for tense-switching. Don't forget to check other elements beyond the main copy, such as captions, page numbers, pull-out quotes, headlines and subheadings. Check contractions too, such as 'won't' and 'can't'. Ask whether they are appropriate for your content. More formal documents will usually feature 'cannot' rather than 'can't'.
— copy ends —

Why machines can't replace proofreaders

Considering how far technology has advanced in the past few years, it's hardly surprising that there are now software packages available that claim to automate the proofreading process. But do they work? Can proofreading software provide an effective shortcut to good text checking?
The only way to find out is to test them. I've chosen eight digital tools. Some of them claim to help you with proofreading, others simply feature spell checking and

grammar policing functionality. The tools are: Grammarly, Ginger, After The Deadline, Style Writer 4.0, Serenity Software's Editor 4.0, Grammarbase.com and the default spell checking talents of Microsoft Word 2010 and Google Drive (formerly Google Docs).

You'll already be familiar with the proofreading test below:

— copy starts —
When Apple Corps launched their first iPhone in 2008, it didn't dissappoint. In fact, it immediately captured the collective imagination with a geeky allure driven by Apples slick design, the phone's smart flexibilty and it's inovative multi-touch approach.
— copy ends —

There are eight mistakes in it – two factual errors ('Apple Corps' and '2008'), three spelling errors ('dissappoint', 'flexibilty' and 'inovative'), and three grammatical errors ('their', 'Apples' and 'it's'). For the purposes of this test, I've discounted the two factual errors, because there's no way that a software program could spot them. That leaves six errors for our auto-proofers to find. So each solution that follows is rated out of six.

Grammarly review

Grammarly.com positions itself as the 'World's Most Accurate Grammar Checker'. It boldly promises to identify over 150 text errors, offer synonym suggestions and to check for plagiarism.

While it's free to get your text checked, you need to sign up for a seven day trial to see what the problems actually are in detail. Beyond the trial, there are a trio of pricing options – you can pay monthly, cough up quarterly or opt for a yearly subscription.

In our proofreading test, Grammarly found five 'issues' with our sample text and instantly identified the three spelling errors – 'dissappoint', 'flexibilty' and 'inovative'. But that was it. It suggested replacing 'didn't' in the sentence: "When Apple Corps launched their first iPhone in 2008, it didn't dissappoint" with 'did not'. And while it highlighted the incorrect use of 'it's' in the final sentence, it suggested 'it has' rather than 'its'.

Grammarly scored: 3/6

Ginger review

Like Grammarly, Ginger touts itself as a do-it-all grammar and spell checker. The big difference is that this downloadable software (PC only) adds proofreading functionality to a number of popular applications – Microsoft Word, Outlook, PowerPoint, Internet Explorer and Firefox.

A small Ginger control bar appears whenever you're actively using a compatible application. You simply click on the bar, or press F2 to start the copy checking process. Ginger then identifies any spelling errors or grammatical mistakes and suggests corrections.

You can test-drive a 600-character demo for free at www.gingersoftware.com/proofreading. The premium version of the software is available for a one-time fee or via a monthly subscription. It's worth it. This version also boasts a clever text-to-speech function, which enables you to hear your text read out loud in a surprisingly decent digital voice. A 'Learning' feature also acts like a virtual tutor, helping you identify common grammatical gaffes and understand how to fix them.

It's a shame then that Ginger had the same success rate as Grammarly, correctly highlighting the three spelling errors, but glossing over the remaining mistakes. Of course, you wouldn't expect a digital tool to get the factual errors in this proofreading test. But the grammar checking isn't all it's cracked up to be either. A spell checker could probably do better...

Ginger scored: 3/6

After The Deadline review

I had high hopes for After The Deadline. You can download it from afterthedeadline.com and use it with bbPress, Confluence and OpenOffice. You can bolt it into Firefox or the Google Chrome browser and you can access it via a WordPress plugin. You can even cut-and-paste the copy you want checked into a web page.

That said, it didn't fare well on this proofreading test. At least not at first. The online version only picked up one of the spelling errors ('flexibilty'), strangely ignoring the other two. And it didn't spot any of the grammatical flaws.

Yet when I tested it again using the WordPress plugin, it picked up all three misspelled words. So if you write content straight into the WordPress dashboard, After The Deadline is useful for making a final pass through your posts in search of spelling errors you might have missed.

After The Deadline scored: 3/6

Style Writer 4.0 review

Style Writer 4.0 is a Microsoft Word plug-in, so you'd expect it to enhance and improve on Microsoft's built-in spelling and grammar checker. Activating it via the 'Add ins' menu, Style Writer 4.0 certainly gives you lots of extra detail about your copy, including rating your sentence length, the reading grade, any passive verb use, as well as how much jargon you've used.

It effortlessly picked up the trio of spelling errors and pointed out the incorrect use of 'it's'. It also suggested editing down 'collective imagination' to improve readability and that 'multi-touch' could be written as one word, like 'multinational'. You can adjust how Style Writer 4.0 analyses text using the Style Categories option.

As impressive as all this is, Style Writer didn't score any higher than Microsoft Word, at least not in this short test. But it's easy to see the reasons for buying it. Find it at www.editorsoftware.com.

Style Writer 4.0 scored: 4/6

Editor 4.0 review

Don't be put off by its 20th century application design, Editor 4.0 from Intelligent Editing enables you to load in a variety of text documents (Word, WordPerfect, Works, HTML, RTF and TXT) and give them a deep spelling check. You can download the Editor from Serenity Software's website and try it free for 10 days.

Whichever version you try, Editor promises to hunt down misspellings, spot mixed cases, incorrect hyphenation, inconsistent US and UK spelling, even highlight potential homonym errors. It can also suggest ways to reduce wordiness and tighten up your copy, point out cliches or vague sentences; target slang words, contractions and potentially misused terms. A separate function will also check for word and phrase repetitions.

So how did it do? It queried the hyphen in 'multi-touch', suggested that 'in fact' could be sliced out to tighten the copy up, and spotted the misused 'it's'. It also picked up the three spelling errors. Test it for yourself at www.serenity-software.com.

Editor 4.0 scored: 4/6

Grammarbase.com review

This free spelling and grammar checking tool can be found online at www.grammarbase.com/check. The website claims that it's 'much more comprehensive than any word processor' and that it checks for 'all types of grammar mistakes, contextual errors, modifiers, prepositions, punctuation, quantifiers, and more.' However, Grammarbase.com only found the three spelling errors in our sample text, missing the grammatical flaws.

Grammarbase.com scored: 3/6

Microsoft Word review

Could a spell checker REALLY do better? Microsoft Word includes spell checking and grammar functionality and so it's interesting to see how the 2010 edition compares to the self-appointed proofreading tools like Grammarly and Ginger.

Quite well, as it turns out. In our proofreading test, Word automatically highlighted the three spelling errors ('dissappoint', 'flexibilty' and 'inovative') in red. It also pointed out the incorrect use of 'it's' (underlining it in blue) and suggesting 'its' as a replacement.

Microsoft Word scored: 4/6

Google Drive review

The document editor in Google Drive (formerly Google Docs) doesn't have a dedicated spelling/grammar check that you can run. But it will highlight incorrectly spelt words and phrases on the fly as you type. In this case, it picked up four of the six errors - the three basic spelling mistakes, plus it was the only auto-proofer to pick up on the missing apostrophe in 'Apples'.

Google Drive scored: 4/6

Proofreading test summary

What we take away from this eight-way match-up is that

you can't beat the eye of a human proofreader. Digital tools can be useful as spell checkers, grammar fixers and synonym suggesters. In some cases, they can help you improve your basic writing skills and steer you away from embarrassing copy editing errors as you create content.

But there's more to proofreading than hunting for typos and making sure you haven't written 'your' when the sentence structure calls for 'you're'.

Digital tools are getting better at spotting contextual errors and punctuation problems, but they're still not an effective substitute for a manual proofreading session. Relying on them is as dangerous as putting your trust in a spell check. We've already seen how they can miss errors that seem obvious to the human eye.

The best solution is still to get somebody else to look over your copy before you publish it and there are a host of online proofreading services for hire. Kibin.com, for example, offers a slick proofreading and editing service with a three-hour turnaround for documents up to 1,000 words. You simply upload your text, choose a delivery time and wait for a Kibin proofreader to tell you when it's done.

5. Proofreading tests

The best way to test your proofreading skills is to try them out with some real-world exercises. On the following pages, you'll find 25 sample tests. Some big, some small. Some have multiple errors, others have only one or two. Remember what you've read so far and consider the common mistakes that people tend to make.

If you'd like PDF versions of these tests, so you can print them out and work on them, then head on over to The Good Content Company website - www.goodcontentcompany.com/proofing-PDFs.

Ready? Then let's get started...

Proofreading test - 'The Roman Baths'

— *copy starts* —

Today, the Roman Baths attracts more than one million visitors a year. It's the city of Bath's premiere tourist attraction – a superbly-preserved Roman bathing house, patched up by some elegant 19th Century re-engineering.

Take a tour and most of the original roman building that stood over 1,900 years ago is still accessible. In fact, when you look down from the Victorian-built terrace to the emerald water in the Great Bath below you're only seeing a small part of the overall site. The Roman Baths are actually 6 metres below the current street level. The rest stretches out underground, beneath nearby streets and the Abbey churchyard.

Bath and North East Somerset Counsel is currently updating the Roman Baths to "keep it at the forefront of the competitive visitor attractions industry." The idea is to look beyond simply showcasing the silent monument and to explore the human story's of the people who used it. Improvements are ongoing. They include new digital photo displays, more detailed scale models, costumed actors, interactive exhibits and virtual 3D reconstructions.

— *copy ends* —

Find the answers to this test in Chapter 6.

Proofreading test #4, part three

Here's the third version of the text excerpt that you should have already read twice by this point. (If you haven't, then you'll find versions one and two mixed into the previous chapter.)

— copy starts —
Editing isn't necessarily about rewriting. It's about tightening text, firming up ideas and polishing presentation. Take out repetitive words where possible and be on the lookout for tense-switching. Don't forget to check other elements beyond the main copy, such as captions, page numbers, pull-out quotes, headlines and subheadings. Check contractions too, such as 'won't' and 'can't'. Ask whether are they appropriate for your content. More formal documents will usually feature 'cannot' rather than 'can't'.
— copy ends —

Did you spot the error? If not, read it back again. There's definitely one there. Find the answer to this test in Chapter 6.

Proofreading test - 'Japanese design'

— copy starts —

It's easy to have preconcieved ideas about Japanese design. On the one hand, Japanese pop culture is infused with a cult of cuteness ('kawaii') that has its roots in the 1970's. Saucer-eyed cartoon characters abound – from international icons like Hello Kitty and pokemon, to the hundreds of lesser-known cartoons designed to sell Japanese snacks and washing powder.

Yet this pervasive Japanese cuteness also collides head on with a harder-edged techno-futurism. This 'Neo-Japan' is defined by its high-tech industrialism – its bullet-nosed Shinkansen trains, exotic robotics and advanced mobile phones. In Tokyo, the Japanese digital lifestyle is immortalised by the neon lights of Akihabara. Here Bic Camera stores sell the latest gadgetry to eager 'otaku' obessed with amine, Manga and videogames.

— copy ends —

How did you do? There were seven mistakes. Find the answers to this test in Chapter 6.

Proofreading test - 'The death of free'

— copy starts —

Could the imminent paywalls around *The Times* and Sunday Times herald the beginning of the end for today's 'free Internet'? It might be tempting to see experiments with paywalls, metered browsing, monthly subscriptions, premium services and micropayments as harbingers of a pay-as-you-go online future. There can be no doubt that the economics of the Internet were shifting and traditional business models are evolving. But will consumers really pay to get access to products, services and information that they currently enjoy for free.

This is precisely the question that a recent Nielsen survey ('Changing Models: A Global Perspective on Paying for Content Online') posed to more than 27,000 consumers across 52 countries. According to the Neilsen data, the vast majority of respondants (85%) think that free content should remain free; 13% had no opinion and 3% disagreed.

— copy ends —

Did you spot all of the mistakes? Find the answers to this test in Chapter 6.

Proofreading test - 'The Dwarves'

— copy starts —

Make a list of all the things you know about dwarves –
braided beards, battle axes, good with hammers, fond of a
beer or two, surnames designed to inspire respect (like
Balendilin Onearm and Giselbert Ironeye), but which
actually give you the giggles. Because as you read the
Dwarves, you can tick these attributes off one-by-one as the
pint-sized Tungdil quests across an evil land to save the
world of Girdlegard from a crazed sorcerer.

Yes, it does sound a little *Lord of the Rings*-y. But it's a
little faster on its feet than Tolkien's classic. Our dwarven
Frodo is Tungdil Bolofar, a bookish dwarf (and part-time
blacksmith) whose been raised in isolation by humans. For
plot's-sake, this means that Tungdil is rubbish at being a
typical dwarf – he's never met another one and can't swing
an axe. So when a army of Àlfar (think dark elves), ogres,
gnomes, kobolds and orcs threaten a full-on fantasy
apocalypse, Tungdil is the least-equipped to do anything
about it. Uprooted from his home, he finds himself
proclaimed the unlikely heir to the dwarven kingdom.

Translated from the German original novel, The
Dwarves often reads like it's been written by an English
student with a new Thesaurus. The high fantasy flourishes
do settle down. But for every inventive set-piece or
dramatic skirmish, there's a silly name to dent the mood –
Nudin the Knowledge-Lusty and Maira the Life Preserver
being two of my favourites. Of course, it's still strangely
readable, chucking in zombies, self-centred wizards,
political bickering and betrayal. It's probably the greatest
dwarf opera since George Lucas finished the script for
Willow.

— copy ends —

Find the answers to this test in Chapter 6.

Proofreading test - 'Aircraft and mobile phones'

— copy starts —

If you believe the aviation industry, your mobile phone has the potential to crash a plane. "Portable telephones and other electronic equipment such as games and computers may interfere with aircraft systems," says British Airways, "and must be switched off during take-off, approach and landing"

But is this actually true? Theoretically, the low-level electromagnetic radiation emitted by a typical GSM phone could have some affect on an aircraft's systems. But crash a plane? Over 150 million passengers flew from BAA's seven UK airports in 2007 and not everyone remembers to turn there phone off.

Because there is no conclusive proof, the aviation industry remains twitchy. On an Alitalia flight in January, three passengers were arrested for refusing to turn their mobile phones. They'll face up to three months in prison for violating safety regulations if found guilty. It's a persuasive argument for switching your phone off, risk or no risk.

Of course, that's not to say that in-flight calling on your phone won't be possible in the future. In December last year, Air France became the first airline in the world to offer the Mobile OnAir system on its AirBus fleet.

OnAir currently allows passengers to send/receive text messages and emails via a mobile phone using GPRS. Communications are handled by a miniature network installed onboard the plane itself. Fully-fledged GSM calling is expected to be added to the Air France service later this year.

— copy ends —

Find the answers to this test in Chapter 6.

Proofreading test - 'System utilities'

— copy starts —

When we talk about 'system utilities', the term describes any software package that is designed specificly to improve and/or maintain the performance and stability of your computer.

There are hundreds of problems that can afflict your computer as you use it. You might not notice them directly, but there might be certain symptoms you've spotted or concerns you might have, such as:

1. Your PC takes more than five minutes to start up

2. Windows performance is sluggish when you open programmes

3. Lack of hard disk space (even though you've deleted unwanted files)

4. You've accidentally lost files and want to recover them

5. You're worried about viruses and spywear

6. You want greater security when using the Internet

6. You realise you haven't backed up your important files

7. You've encountered a 'registry' error and don't know how to fix it

System utilities can solve all of the seven problems above and key benefits include speeding up the overall performance of your computerm and cleaning your hard disk drive of unwanted software.

Is your computer running slowly and you don't know why? Then Iolo System Mechanic can give it a kick. Maybe your PC crashes unexpectedly? A package like System Suite 10 Professional can potentially identify damaging problems and eliminate them.

That's not all these powerful products can do for you.

They can also fix hundreds of Windows errors, free up disk space, back up your important files, even unearth problems you didn't know you had, like lurking viruses and malware.

They can do all this automatically too. Just put your feet up and, with a few clicks of your mouse, you can launch a comprehensive IT health check that could keep your computer running as smoothly as the day you brought it.

— copy ends —

Did you spot the seven errors in the text? Find the answers to this test in Chapter 6.

Proofreading test - 'SS Great Britain'

— copy starts —

Isambard Kingdom Brunel had a grand vision. Working for the Great Western Steamship Company, his idea was to extend the reach of the Great Western Railway to New York. Passengers would be able to travel from London to Bristol by train, stay in a hotel overnight, before boarding the luxurious SS Great Britain for the Transatlantic journey the next day. All on one ticket.

Sadly, the SS Great Britain never carried passengers from Bristol and it was never quite the success that Brunell or the GWSSC hoped it would be. Instead, the SS Great Britain sailed from Liverpool between 1845 and 1846, before running aground off the coast of Northern Eireland and bankrupting its owners. Stranded for almost a year, Brunel's leviathan ship was finally refloated and sold on to Gibbs Bright & Co who had very different plans for her.

Abandoning the transatlantic route, Gibbs Bright & Co refitted the SS Great Britain to carry immigrants to Melbourne, Australia. They replaced the propeller, the udder, and swapped out Brunel's original engine with a more efficient model. An extra deck was also added, boosting the capacity from 252 first- and second-class passengers to over 700.

— copy ends —

Find the answers to this test in Chapter 6.

Proofreading test - 'How to save a wet phone'

— copy starts —

Whether you've dunked your phone in the sink, dropped it down the the toilet, or left it in a coat pocket through a 40 degree wash and two spins, there's still an chance that you can save it. But you need to act quickly. Follow these six steps.

Step 1: Turn your phone off

Most phones can survive a brief dunking, so retrieve your phone and quickly turn it off. If you can, remove the battery and extract the SIM module. This will cut the power to the delicate electronics and safeguard your contacts.

Step 2: Mop up the water you CAN see

The key to saving a wet phone is to dry it out quickly. Take your phone apart as far as you can without using a screwdriver. Then grab some paper towels or use your clothes to clean off the surface water.

Step 3: remove the water you CAN'T see

Use gentle heat or blasts of air to dry your phone's innards. You can also use a hairdryer (on a low heat) too, but don't hold it closer than about 12 inches. You don't want to risk the components getting warped as they dry. Don't put it on a radiator either. Or in a microwave. Sucking the water out with a vacuum cleaner can also prove affective.

Step 4: Leave it in an airing cupboard

Leave your damp mobile somewhere warm for a couple of days to fully dry out. You could also try leaving it in a big bowl of uncooked rice which apparantly helps absorb moisture.

Step 5: Try switching it back on

Reconnect the battery and try switching your phone back on. If it works, we recommend getting a new battery - your original one could be damaged.

— copy ends —

Can you find the errors in this proofreading test? Check your answers to this test in Chapter 6.

Proofreading test - 'Playing the piano'

— copy starts —

Robert Donlan began playing the piano at the age of four. Both of his parents played in an orchestra and the house was always filled with music, from Dvorak's toe-tapping Slavonic Dances to Tchaikovsky's stirring symphonies. As his family couldn't afford a piano, nor had the space to accomodate one, Doolan used to go to his Uncle John's and Auntie Sue's house to practice. He remembers those days fondly, but eventually got his own piano when his family moved to a bigger house in 1982. "It was an old-fashioned Waldstein 108 upright," he recalls. "I fell in love with it immediately."

— copy ends —

Find the answers to this test in Chapter 6.

Proofreading test - 'The ambassador'

— copy starts —

The new ambassador bowed before the Duke. He complemented His Excellency on the party and on the venue. The view from the windows across the bay, with the snow-capped peek towering beyond it, was a truly magnificent site. At the same time, he preyed that the ambassador wouldn't notice the cheep suit that he was wearing. He hadnt had the time to buy anything better. The Duke shook his hand warmly, wasting no time in brooching the subject of the council meeting later that night.

— copy ends —

Find the answers to this test in Chapter 6.

Proofreading test - 'Fantasy'

— copy starts —

King Annolt heaved himself out of the chair and strode across to the old painting that hung on the wall. He looked up at his father leading a calvary charge, trampling over the fallen bodies of his enemies, his arm victoriously held a loft, the tribal banner trailing from his fist. Muscled and hansome gods watched approvingly from the clouds above, illuminating the battlefield with golden rays of holy light. This is what glory looked like. Annolt knew every detail of the picture. He could see himself in his father's place. He had the same armour. He wore the same crown. He was every inch the hero his father had been. A few more inches around the waist, perhaps. But heroic nonetheless.

— copy ends —

You'll find the answers to this proofreading test in Chapter 6.

Proofreading test - 'Mirror, mirror'

— copy starts —
"Mirror, mirror on the wall, who is the fairest of them all?"
— copy ends —

Can you spot the mistake? Find the answer to this test in Chapter 6.

Proofreading test - 'Wine'

— copy starts —

On our next visit, we are greeted by the manager and taken on an hour-long tour of the vine yard. It was one of the most beuatiful places which I've ever seen. Beneath a cobalt-blue sky, row upon row of chardonnay, syrah and merlot vines curved across the valley floor towards a ruined roman-style chapel. The towering mountains in the distance gave the whole scene extra grandeure. I rememember that The air was pleasantly warm and surprisingly still. The conditions were perfect for growing grapes. It's was easy to understand why the owner, Simon Booth, and his family had settled there.

— copy ends —

Find the answers to this test in Chapter 6.

Proofreading test - 'Paris in a weekend'

— copy starts —
Paris in a weekend

The creme de la creme of the french capital is only a train ride away. Here are our top five places to visit...

1. Eiffel Tower
The best views from the Eiffel Tower are from the second stage, so you don't need to go all the way to the top. Try visiting at night to see a breathtaking vista of lights or get a great view of the tower during the day from the Pallais de Chaillot, near the Trocadéro metro station. Buy your ticket in advance online to avoid lengthy queues.
2. Notre Dame
Did you know that this must-see Gothic cathedral took 200 years to build? Located on the banks of the Seine, it's an extraordinary sight, inside and out. Feeling fit? You can climb the 387 steps to the bell tower for a superb view of the french capital. Our tip: queue for the bell tower first and get in line by 9am.
3. Montmartre
Montmartre is the highest hill in Paris and it's here that you'll find the famous Sacré Coeur basillica. While the Sacré Coeur gets crowded at weekends, take time to explore the side streets, where you'll find hidden gems like the garden of the Montmartre museum. If you don't fancy walking, take Le Petit Train de Montmartre which departs opposite the Moulin Rouge.
4. Musée d'Orsay
Housed in a former railway station, this fascinating museum is home to a stunning collection of impressionist and post-impressionist art. Here you'll find paintings by Monet, Degas, Gauguin and Van Gogh. Arrive early to avoid the queues. Weekdays are less crowded.

5. The Louvre

This is France's most famous museum, its entranceway marked by an iconic glass pyramid. It's a huge museum, you'll probably never see everything. So plan your trip in advance and target the key areas you want to see. It's a good idea to buy tickets in advance from ww.louvre.fr or to buy a museum pass. Café Mollien on the first floor is perfect for a snack. Sit on the terrace and enjoy the view over the Cour Napoléon.

— *copy ends* —

You'll find the answers and corrections for this test in Chapter 6.

Proofreading test - 'Nokia Lumia 920 vs Google Nexus 4'

— copy starts —

The innards of the impressive Nokia Lumia 920 come packed with NFC, 3G/HSDPA, 802.11a/b/g/n Wi-Fi and Bluetoot 3.1 with A2DP. It also boasts 4G connectivty where available. As for the Nexus 4 handset, LG has built it for Google with NFC, 3G/HSPDA, Bluetooth 4.0 with A2DP and 802.1a/b/g/n Wi-Fi baked in as standard. There's no 4G here though, which is a shame.

The Lumia 920 also sports a 8.0 Megapixel camera (with autofocus, a dual LED flash, Carl Zeiss optics, Nokia's own PureView technology, touch focus, image stablization and 1080p video recording. So there's no real difference in raw megapixels. A second 1.3 Megapixel camera on the front can be used for video calling.

— copy ends —

How many mistakes did you spot? By my count, there are eight. Check the answers to this test in Chapter 6.

Proofreading test - 'Weather vane'

— copy starts —

He tried in vane to fix the weather vane. The blood pumped through his vanes as he banged the hammer down on the dented metal. "Must... Fix... The... Vane," he muttered. "He... Can't... Find... Out..." With each ear-splitting blow, the bent metal vane clattered and clanged on the old anvil. His dad would never understand. This was a vane attempt to avoid an argument. The new iron ore vane they'd discovered in the far field last week wouldn't keep him busy for long.

— copy ends —

Find the answers to this test in Chapter 6.

Proofreading test - 'Star-spangled'

— copy starts —
O say can you see by the dawns early light,
What so proudly we hailed at the twilights last gleaming,
Whose broad stripes and bright stars through the perilous fight,
Oer the ramparts we watched, were so gallantly streaming
And the rockets red glare, the bombs bursting in air,
Gave proof through the night that our flag was still there;
O say does that star-spangled banner yet wave,
Oer the land of the free and the home of the brave
— copy ends —

Find the answers to this test in Chapter 6.

Proofreading test - 'Penny Lane'

— copy starts —
In Penny Lane there is a barber showing photographs
Of every head he's had the pleasure to know.
And all the people that come and go,
Stop and say "hello".

On the corner is a banker with a motorcar,
The little children laugh at him behind his back.
And the banker never wears a mac,
In the pouring rain, very strange.

Penny Lane is in my ears and in my eyes.
There beneath the blue surburban skies
I sit, and meanwhile back

In Penny Lane there is a fireman with an hourglass.
And in his pocket is a portrait of the Queen.
He likes to keep his fire engine clean,
It's a clean machine.
— copy ends —

Find the answers to this test in Chapter 6.

Proofreading test - 'The Manor'

— copy starts —

Come and see a very unique collaboration with students from Bucks New University. *Sculpture in the Park* is a series of large outdoor artworks inspired by the the history and surroundings of Hughenden Manor. From August to September, you can hear short talks from costumed characters in costume about what life was like at the house during the mid-1800's. Finally, if you're visiting us in December, enjoy the holiday season with atmospheric victorian show rooms decorated in traditional style. Plus there's plenty of family fun and ideas for Christmas gifts!!

— copy ends —

Find the answers to this test in Chapter 6.

Proofreading test - '30,000 trees'

— copy starts —

Ever since Hurricane Catrina battered New Orleans, the US Army Corps of Engineers has enforced vegetation removal on levies across the United States. But recent research has shown that trees can actually help to reinforce and strengthen these artificial walls. Consequently, the Corps has started to plant over 30,000 trees along the Sacramento River, as part of the $180 million dollar repairs to those levies that were overwhelmed by flooding. The Corps aims to do the planting between December 2012 and March 2012. It will hire a contractor and does not yet have a cost estimate.

— copy ends —

How many mistakes did you spot? By my count, there are five. Check the answers to this test in Chapter 6.

Proofreading test - 'Texting'

— copy starts —
We asked 100 London children how they communicate with their friends after school hours. Most admitted that they send texts or instant messages to their friends using their mobile phones. According to the survey, the four principle channels for this communication are: BlackBerry Messenger (BBM), Facebook and SMS messaging. 10 years ago this question would have illicited a very different response.
— copy ends —

Can you find the errors in this proofreading test? Find the answers in Chapter 6.

Proofreading Test - 'Boors'

— *copy starts* --

Can you believe it? We're going on a boor hunt today.
A boor hunt! They're wild pigs, I believe. It doesn't matter,
because I strongly disagree with this so-called 'sport' and I
don't like our host. I don't care if he does own half of
Oxfordshire. The man is relentlessly borish. In fact, the
whole weekend bores me. I'd much rather let the poor boor
roam free and spend my time at home with a good book.

— *copy ends* —

Find the answers to this test in Chapter 6.

Proofreading test - 'Quick snaps'

— copy starts —

Most people take their digital cameras with them when they go on holiday or shoot quick snaps on the mobile phones. But, more often then not, the results can be dissappointing. This is either because most cameras aren't set up correctly the subject is poorly framed or the flash is set to Automatic when it should be Disabled. Fortunately, a few simple techniques can help you take better photos the next time you travel.

— copy ends —

Find the answers to this test in Chapter 6.

Proofreading test - 'Murder'

— copy starts —

"Yes, I was on the trip to south America, as was Mr Carmichael and Doctor Jarratt. Why do you ask?"

The policeman flipped open his notebook. "Did you happen to meet a Mr Jonathan Hart at any point?"

"Actually, yes. He dined at our table on our first night at see. He worked for an oil company, I think. Why do you ask?".

"Because Mr Hart was murdered," said the policeman flatly. "And you were one of the last people to see him alive."

"You have a flare for the dramatic, officer. What can I do to help?"

— copy ends —

Find the answers to this test in Chapter 6.

Proofreading test - 'Ooh, oh, ah'

— copy starts —

Before every convert performance, Zack warms up his vocal chords with a series of simple singing exercises. The idea is to relax his throat and release any built-up tension in the muscles. He says that his routine hasn't changed since his first appearance at the Royal Albert Hall. He starts with some neck rolls, followed by a series of shoulder rolls, before launching into a gentle set of half-scales using vowel sounds ("ooh", "oh", "ah', "ee" and "eh").

— copy ends —

How did you do? There were three mistakes. Find the corrections and answers to this test in Chapter 6.

Proofreading test - 'Frost'

— copy starts —

Richard Frost was at the peak of his physical fitness and his excellent racing results had peaked the interest of the national cycling coach. On the Thursday after Easter, the coach decided to take a peak at Richard's punishing training regime, which involved a challenging mountain peak climb, followed by a fast descent into the valley below.

— copy ends —

Find the answers to this test in Chapter 6.

6. Proofreading test answers

Answers - 'The Roman Baths'

— copy starts —

Today, the Roman Baths attracts more than one million visitors a year. It's the **city** of Bath's **premiere** tourist attraction – a superbly-preserved Roman bathing house, patched up by some elegant 19th Century re-engineering.

Take a tour and most of the original **roman** building that stood over 1,900 years ago is still accessible. In fact, when you look down from the Victorian-built terrace to the emerald water in the Great Bath below you're only seeing a small part of the overall site. The Roman Baths are actually **6 metres** below the current street level. The rest stretches out underground, beneath nearby streets and the Abbey churchyard.

Bath and North East Somerset **Counsel** is currently updating the Roman Baths to "keep it at the forefront of the competitive visitor attractions industry." The idea is to look beyond simply showcasing the silent monument and to explore the human **story's** of the people who used it. Improvements are ongoing. They include new digital photo displays, more detailed scale models, costumed actors, interactive exhibits and virtual 3D reconstructions.

— copy ends —

city: In the phrase City of Bath, 'city' has a capital 'C' as it's part of the name.

premiere: It should be 'premier'; 'premiere' means 'the first public performance of a movie or play'.

roman: this references the 'Roman empire' and a historical period. Therefore it should be capped.

6: Numbers between 0-9 should be written out in full. So this should be 'six'.

Counsel: This should be 'Council'. 'Counsel' means to 'give advice'.

story's: Incorrect use of an apostrophe to indicate a

plural. The word we're looking for here is 'stories'.

Answers - Proofreading test #4

— copy starts —

Editing isn't necessarily about rewriting. It's about tightening text, firming up ideas and polishing presentation. Take out repetitive words where possible and be on the lookout for tense-switching. Don't forget to check other elements beyond the main copy, such as captions, page numbers, pull-out quotes, headlines and subheadings. Check contractions too, such as 'won't' and 'can't'. **Ask whether are they** appropriate for your content. More formal documents will usually feature 'cannot' rather than 'can't'.

— copy ends —

Ask whether are they: It should be 'Ask whether they are...' Often a simple mistake like two switched words can be overlooked, especially if you have become familiar with the content. When content is familiar, you can't help but anticipate what comes next. Consequently, you find yourself proofreading faster because, at the back of your mind, you know that you've read these words before and there was nothing wrong with them before. It's this subconscious lack of attention that can cause errors to slip through.

Answers - 'Japanese design'

— copy starts —

It's easy to have **preconcieved** ideas about Japanese design. On the one hand, Japanese pop culture is infused with a cult of cuteness ('kawaii') that has its roots in the **1970's**. Saucer-eyed cartoon characters abound – from international icons like Hello Kitty and **pokemon**, to the hundreds of lesser-known cartoons designed to sell Japanese snacks and washing powder.

Yet this pervasive Japanese cuteness also collides **head on** with a harder-edged techno-futurism. This 'Neo-Japan' is defined by its high-tech industrialism – its bullet-nosed Shinkansen trains, exotic robotics and advanced mobile phones. In Tokyo, the Japanese digital lifestyle is immortalised by the neon lights of Akihabara. Here Bic Camera stores sell the latest gadgetry to eager 'otaku' **obessed** with **amine**, **Manga** and videogames.

— copy ends —

preconcieved: Transposed letters are one of the most common spelling errors that you'll find in your copy. The correct spelling is 'preconceived'. As the rhyme goes - 'I before E, except after C'.

1970's: It's 1970s. There's no apostrophe needed here.

pokemon: Pokemon is a brand name and so should have a capital 'P'.

head on: While there's no spelling error here, the two words should be hyphenated - 'head-on'

obessed: Note the missing 's' - 'obsessed'.

amine: It should be 'anime'. An 'amine' is an organic compound that contains a basic nitrogen atom.

Manga: There's no capital letter on either 'anime' or 'manga'. They are artistic styles and both common nouns, like 'romance' and 'mystery'.

Answers - 'The death of free'

— copy starts —

Could the imminent paywalls around **The Times** and **Sunday Times** herald the beginning of the end for today's 'free Internet'? It might be tempting to see experiments with paywalls, metered browsing, monthly subscriptions, premium services and micropayments as harbingers of a pay-as-you-go online future. There can be no doubt that the economics of the Internet **were** shifting and traditional business models are evolving. But will consumers really pay to get access to products, services and information that they currently enjoy for **free.**

This is precisely the question that a recent Nielsen survey ('Changing Models: A Global Perspective on Paying for Content Online') posed to more than 27,000 consumers across 52 countries. According to the **Neilsen** data, the vast majority of **respondants** (85%) think that free content should remain free; 13% had no opinion and **3%** disagreed.

— copy ends —

The Times: If you are making a conscious decision to use italics to indicate media publications, then the 'Sunday Times' should also be italicised. If not, consistency demands that neither newspaper is.

were shifting: There's a shift in tenses in this sentence from present to past. It should say 'are shifting'.

free: Missing question mark. This sentence asks a question.

Neilsen: Again, we're aiming for consistent spelling. 'Nielsen' is the correct spelling, so 'Neilsen' is incorrect here.

respondants: 'respondents'.

3%: If you add up the percentages here, you'll see that the total is 101%. This means one of the figures is wrong. If you're the writer, you can easily change it. If not, there's no easy way to tell. Contact the author of the content for clarification.

Answers - 'The Dwarves'

— copy starts —

Make a list of all the things you know about dwarves –
braided beards, battle axes, good with hammers, fond of a
beer or two, surnames designed to inspire respect (like
Balendilin Onearm and Giselbert Ironeye), but which
actually give you the giggles. Because as you read **the
Dwarves**, you can tick these attributes off one-by-one as
the pint-sized Tungdil quests across an evil land to save the
world of Girdlegard from a crazed sorcerer.

Yes, it does sound a little *Lord of the Rings*-y. But it's a
little faster on its feet than Tolkien's classic. Our dwarven
Frodo is Tungdil Bolofar, a bookish dwarf (and part-time
blacksmith) **whose** been raised in isolation by humans. For
plot's-sake, this means that Tungdil is terrible at being a
typical dwarf – he's never met another one and can't swing
an axe. So when **a army** of Àlfar (think dark elves), ogres,
gnomes, kobolds and orcs **threaten** a full-on fantasy
apocalypse, Tungdil is the least-equipped to do anything
about it. Uprooted from his home, he finds himself
proclaimed the unlikely heir to the dwarven kingdom.

Translated from the **German original novel**, The
Dwarves often reads like it's been written by an English
student with a new Thesaurus. The high fantasy flourishes
do settle down. But for every inventive set-piece or
dramatic skirmish, there's a silly name to dent the mood –
Nudin the Knowledge-Lusty and Maira the Life Preserver
being two of my favourites. Of course, it's still strangely
readable, chucking in zombies, self-centred wizards,
political bickering and betrayal. It's probably the greatest
dwarf opera since George Lucas finished the script for
Willow.

— copy ends —

the Dwarves: This is the title of the book and should be written with caps - 'The Dwarves'.

whose: It should be 'who's', the contracted form of 'who has'

a army: 'an army'

threaten: Who's doing the threatening here? It's the army. Singular. Not the ogres, gnomes, kobolds and orcs. Therefore it needs to say 'threatens'.

German original novel: incorrect word order - 'original German novel'

Willow: As *Lord of the Rings* was italicised earlier in the text, *Willow* should also be italicised for consistency.

Answers - 'Aircraft & mobile phones'

— copy starts —

If you believe the aviation industry, your mobile phone has the potential to crash a plane. "Portable telephones and other electronic equipment such as games and computers may interfere with aircraft systems," says British Airways, "and must be switched off during take-off, approach and **landing"**

But is this actually true? Theoretically, the low-level electromagnetic radiation emitted by a typical GSM phone could have some **affect** on an aircraft's systems. But crash a plane? Over 150 million passengers flew from BAA's seven UK airports in 2007 and not everyone remembers to turn **there** phone off.

Because there is no conclusive proof, the aviation industry remains twitchy. On an Alitalia flight in January, three passengers were arrested for refusing to **turn their mobile phones**. They'll face up to three months in prison for violating safety regulations if found guilty. It's a persuasive argument for switching your phone off, risk or no risk.

Of course, that's not to say that in-flight calling on your phone won't be possible in the future. In December last year, Air France became the first airline in the world to offer the Mobile OnAir system on its **AirBus** fleet.

OnAir currently allows passengers to send/receive text messages and emails via a mobile phone using GPRS. Communications are handled by a miniature network installed onboard the plane itself. Fully-fledged GSM calling is expected to be added to the Air France service later this year.

— copy ends —

landing": missing full stop.
affect: 'effect'

there: 'their'

Turn their mobile phones: 'turn off their mobile phones'

AirBus: 'Airbus'

Answers - 'System utilities'

— copy starts —

When we talk about 'system utilities', the term describes any software package that is designed **specificly** to improve and/or maintain the performance and stability of your computer.

There are hundreds of problems that can afflict your computer as you use it. You might not notice them directly, but there might be certain symptoms you've spotted or concerns you might have, such as:

1. Your PC takes more than five minutes to start up
2. Windows performance is sluggish when you open **programmes**
3. Lack of hard disk space (even though you've deleted unwanted files)
4. You've accidentally lost files and want to recover them
5. You're worried about viruses and **spywear**
6. You want greater security when using the Internet
6. **You realise you haven't backed up your important files**
7. You've encountered a 'registry' error and don't know how to fix it

System utilities can solve all of the **seven problems** above and key benefits include speeding up the overall performance of your **computerm** and cleaning your hard disk drive of unwanted software.

Is your computer running slowly and you don't know why? Then Iolo System Mechanic can give it a kick. Maybe your PC crashes unexpectedly? A package like System Suite 10 Professional can potentially identify damaging problems and eliminate them.

That's not all these powerful products can do for you.

They can also fix hundreds of Windows errors, free up disk space, back up your important files, even unearth problems you didn't know you had, like lurking viruses and malware.

They can do all this automatically too. Just put your feet up and, with a few clicks of your mouse, you can launch a comprehensive IT health check that could keep your computer running as smoothly as the day you **brought** it.

— *copy ends* —

specificly: A spell check will easily catch this error, but it might be difficult to see if you're proofreading too quickly. 'Specifically'.

programmes: In British English, 'programme' is used to describe plans, schedules and shows. The correct spelling is 'program'.

spywear: We don't fear black body suits and balaclavas. We fear 'spyware', which can snoop on our keystrokes and steal our passwords.

6. You realise you haven't backed up your important files: This should be numbered '7' and the following point numbered '8'.

seven problems: The incorrect labelling of the list means that it's easy to write 'seven problems' when there are actually 'eight'.

computerm: Again, a spell check should catch this odd error. Extra letters can often get added to words when you're editing and you mistype. Watch out for this and always re-check a sentence you've edited or re-run a spell check.

brought: 'bought'

132

Answers - 'SS Great Britain'

— copy starts —

Isambard Kingdom Brunel had a grand vision. Working for the Great Western Steamship Company, his idea was to extend the reach of the Great Western Railway to New York. Passengers would be able to travel from London to Bristol by train, stay in a hotel overnight, before boarding the luxurious SS Great Britain for the **Transatlantic** journey the next day. All on one ticket.

Sadly, the SS Great Britain never carried passengers from Bristol and it was never quite the success that **Brunell** or the **GWSSC** hoped it would be. Instead, the SS Great Britain sailed from Liverpool between 1845 and 1846, before running aground off the coast of Northern **Eireland** and bankrupting its owners. Stranded for almost a year, Brunel's leviathan ship was finally refloated and sold on to Gibbs Bright & Co who had very different plans for her.

Abandoning the transatlantic route, Gibbs Bright & Co refitted the SS Great Britain to carry **immigrants** to Melbourne, Australia. They replaced the propeller, the **udder**, and swapped out Brunel's original engine with a more efficient model. An extra deck was also added, boosting the capacity from 252 first- and second-class passengers to over 700.

— copy ends —

Transatlantic: This word doesn't need a capital 'T'. It is simply 'transatlantic'.

Brunell: Watch out for inconsistent spelling of people, places, companies and products. Brunel has one 'l', not two.

GWSSC: This is the wrong acronym for the Great Western Steamship Company. It should be GWSC.

Eireland: The correct spelling is, of course, 'Ireland'.

immigrants: No spelling error here, but the wrong word entirely. To say the ship was carrying 'immigrants'

133

suggests that it was transporting foreigners who had previously settled in Britain. The SS Great Britain carried 'emigrants', British residents who wanted to settle abroad.

udder: 'rudder'

Answers - 'How to save a wet phone'

— copy starts —

Whether you've dunked your phone in the sink, dropped it **down the the toilet**, or left it in a coat pocket through a 40 degree wash and two spins, there's **still an chance** that you can save it. But you need to act quickly. Follow these **six** steps.

Step 1: Turn your phone off

Most phones can survive a brief dunking, so retrieve your phone and quickly turn it off. If you can, remove the battery and extract the **SIM module**. This will cut the power to the delicate electronics and safeguard your contacts.

Step 2: Mop up the water you CAN see

The key to saving a wet phone is to dry it out quickly. Take your phone apart as far as you can without using a screwdriver. Then grab some paper towels or use your clothes to clean off the surface water.

Step 3: **remove** the water you CAN'T see

Use gentle heat or blasts of air to dry your phone's innards. You can **also** use a hairdryer (on a low heat) **too**, but don't hold it closer than about 12 inches. You don't want to risk the components getting warped as they dry. Don't put it on a radiator either. Or in a microwave. Sucking the water out with a vacuum cleaner can also prove **affective**.

Step 4: Leave it in an airing cupboard

Leave your damp mobile somewhere warm for a couple of days to fully dry out. You could also try leaving it in a big bowl of uncooked rice **which apparantly** helps absorb moisture.

Step 5: Try switching it back on

Reconnect the battery and try switching your phone back on. If it works, we recommend getting a new battery -

your original one could be damaged.

— copy ends —

down the the toilet: There's a double 'the' here. Most spell checkers will catch this, but don't take that chance.

still an chance: This should read: 'still a chance'

six steps: There are only five steps. Perhaps there were six steps in an earlier version of the copy and one was deleted without updating the reference.

SIM module: 'SIM' stands for 'Subscriber Identity Module' or 'Subscriber Identification Module', so you don't need the word 'module' that follows it here.

remove: There should be a capital 'R'.

also/too: You don't need both of these words, just the one will do.

affective: 'effective'

which apparantly: There are two errors here. First, with a 'which' present in the sentence, there should be a comma after 'rice' - 'uncooked rice, which...' Second, 'apparantly' is spelt incorrectly. It should be 'apparently'. Did you get both errors? It's easy to focus on the more obvious spelling error at the expense of the grammatical mistake.

Answers - 'Playing the piano'

— copy starts —

Robert Donlan began playing the piano at the age of four. Both of his parents played in an orchestra and the house was always filled with music, from Dvorak's toe-tapping Slavonic Dances to Tchaikovsky's stirring symphonies. As his family couldn't afford a piano, nor had the space to **accomodate** one, **Doolan** used to go to his **Uncle John's and Auntie Sue's** house to **practice**. He remembers those days fondly, but eventually got his own piano when his family moved to a bigger house in 1982. "It was an old-fashioned Waldstein 108 upright," Donlan recalls. "I fell in love with it immediately."

— copy ends —

accomodate: 'accommodate'

Doolan: The subject of the article has been introduced as 'Robert Donlan', so the mention of 'Doolan' here is incorrect.

Uncle John's and Auntie Sue's: There is one too many apostrophes here. As there's one house, we can say 'Uncle John and Auntie Sue's'. If Uncle John and Auntie Sue had sadly split up and lived in separate houses, we'd write 'Uncle John's and Auntie Sue's houses'.

practice: 'Practice' is a noun, 'you go to piano practice'. We want 'practise' in this instance - 'to practise'.

Answers - 'The ambassador'

— copy starts —

The ambassador bowed before the Duke. He **complemented** His Excellency on the party and on the venue. The view from the windows across the bay, with the snow-capped **peek** towering beyond it, was a truly magnificent **site**. At the same time, he **preyed** that the ambassador wouldn't notice the **cheep** suit that he was wearing. He **hadnt** had the time to buy anything better. The Duke shook the ambassador's hand warmly, wasting no time in **brooching** the subject of the council meeting later that night.

— copy ends —

complemented: This is the first of many homophone errors. It should be 'complimented'.

peek: 'Peek' means to 'glance at', 'peak' is the summit of a mountain.

site: 'Site' means 'place' or 'location', 'sight' describes a 'view'

preyed: The word we need here is 'prayed'. 'Preyed' means 'hunted'.

cheep: The sound a baby chick makes. Whereas 'cheap' describes something that is 'inexpensive'.

hadnt: The only mistake that's not a homophone error. It's missing an apostrophe. 'Hadn't' is short for 'had not'.

brooching: 'Brooch' is a decorative piece of jewellery, 'broach' means 'to mention for the first time'.

Answers - 'Fantasy'

— copy starts —

King Annolt heaved himself out of the chair and strode across to the old painting that hung on the wall. He looked up at his father leading a **calvary** charge, trampling over the fallen bodies of his enemies, his arm victoriously held **a loft**, the tribal banner trailing from his fist. Muscled and **hansome** gods watched approvingly from the clouds above, illuminating the battlefield with golden rays of holy light. This is what glory looked like. Annolt knew every detail of the picture. He could see himself in his father's place. He had the same armour. He wore the same crown. He was every inch the hero his father had been. A few more inches around the waist, perhaps. But heroic nonetheless.

— copy ends —

calvary: Also known as Golgotha, 'Calvary' is acknowledged as the place outside the walls of Jerusalem, where Jesus was crucified. 'Cavalry' refers to warriors/soldiers who fight on horseback. The two words look very similar.

a loft: 'aloft' is one word.

hansome: It's 'handsome'. Note the silent 'd'.

Answers - 'Mirror, mirror'

— copy starts —
"Mirror, mirror on the wall, who is the fairest of them all?"
— copy ends —

"Mirror, mirror on the wall, who is the fairest of them all?": This was a bit of a sneaky one, more of a copy editing test than a proofreading one. The quote as written here might sound familiar, but the Queen never said this line in the 1937 Disney movie. The real quote was: "Magic Mirror, on the wall, who is the fairest one of all?" It's an interesting lesson in taking things for granted and a reminder to always check facts.

Answers - 'Wine'

— copy starts —

On our next visit, we **are** greeted by the manager and taken on an hour-long tour of the **vine yard**. It was one of the most **beuatiful** places **which** I've ever seen. Beneath a cobalt-blue sky, row upon row of **chardonnay, syrah and merlot** vines curved across the valley floor towards a ruined **roman**-style chapel. The towering mountains in the distance gave the whole scene extra **grandeure**. I **rememember** that **The air** was pleasantly warm and surprisingly still. The conditions were perfect for growing grapes. **It's was** easy to understand why the owner, Simon Booth, and his family had settled there.

— copy ends —

are: wrong tense, but you only realise it when you've read further into the copy. So you need to go back and change it to 'were'.

vine yard: 'vineyard' is one word.

beuatiful: Sometimes when you type too quickly, you can transpose letters and create mistakes that can be hard to spot at-a-glance. The correct spelling here is, of course, 'beautiful'.

which: In this context, the correct word is 'that'. Using 'which' doesn't make sense.

chardonnay, syrah and merlot: These are all grape varieties and should be capitalised.

roman: Again, we're talking about an historical era, so this should be 'Roman'.

grandeure: 'grandeur'

rememember: There are too many 'm's in this spelling of 'remember'.

The air: Did you spot the misplaced capital letter here?

It's was: 'It was'

Answers - 'Paris in a weekend'

— copy starts —
Paris in a weekend

The creme de la creme of the **french** capital is only a train ride away. Here are our top five places to visit...

1. Eiffel Tower

The best views from the Eiffel Tower are from the second stage, so you don't need to go all the way to the top. Try visiting at night to see a breathtaking vista of lights or get a great view of the tower during the day from the **Pallais de Chaillot**, near the Trocadéro metro station. Buy your ticket in advance online to avoid lengthy queues.

2. Notre Dame

Did you know that this must-see Gothic cathedral took 200 years to build? Located on the banks of the Seine, it's an extraordinary sight, inside and out. Feeling fit? You can climb the 387 steps to the bell tower for a superb view of the **french** capital. Our tip: queue for the bell tower first and get in line by 9am.

3. Montmartre

Montmartre is the highest hill in Paris and it's here that you'll find the famous Sacré Coeur **basillica**. While the Sacré Coeur gets crowded at weekends, take time to explore the side streets, where you'll find hidden gems like the garden of the Montmartre museum. If you don't fancy walking, take Le Petit Train de **Montmartre which** departs opposite the Moulin Rouge.

4. Musée d'Orsay

Housed in a former railway station, this fascinating museum is home to a stunning collection of **impressionist** and post-**impressionist** art. Here you'll find paintings by Monet, Degas, Gauguin and Van Gogh. Arrive early to avoid the queues. Weekdays are less crowded.

5. The Louvre

This is France's most famous museum, its entranceway marked by an iconic glass pyramid. It's a huge museum, you'll probably never see everything. So plan your trip in advance and target the key areas you want to see. It's a good idea to buy tickets in advance from **ww.louvre.fr** or to buy a museum pass. Café Mollien on the first floor is perfect for a snack. Sit on the terrace and enjoy the view over the Cour Napoléon.

— *copy ends* —

french: This error appears twice in the text. It should be capped-up, 'French'

Pallais de Chaillot: Even though you're dealing with foreign place names, it's always worth checking the spelling just to be sure that there are no silly mistakes. Here, for example, 'Pallais' is incorrect. The correct spelling of the word is 'Palais'.

basillica: 'basilica', single 'l'. Errors like this can be hard to spot if you're proofreading text in a small font. The 'l's blur together and you might not spot the extra one.

Montmartre which: This should be changed to either 'Montmartre, which' (adding a comma), or to 'Montmartre that'.

impressionist: When we're talking about the 19th century art movement, we should capitalise the 'I'. So it's correct to write 'Impressionism' and 'Impressionist'.

ww.louvre.fr: There's a missing 'w' in this web address. It should read 'www.louvre.fr'.

Answers - 'Nokia Lumia 920 vs Google Nexus 4'

— copy starts —

The innards of the impressive Nokia Lumia 920 come packed with NFC, 3G/HSDPA, 802.11a/b/g/n Wi-Fi and **Bluetoot** 3.1 with A2DP. It also boasts 4G **connectivty** where available. As for the Nexus 4 handset, LG has built it for Google with NFC, **3G/HSPDA**, Bluetooth 4.0 with A2DP and **802.1a/b/g/n** Wi-Fi baked in as standard. There's no 4G here though, which is a shame.

The Lumia 920 also sports **a 8.0 Megapixel** camera **(with autofocus**, a dual LED flash, Carl Zeiss optics, Nokia's own PureView technology, touch focus, image **stablization** and 1080p video recording. So there's no real difference in raw **megapixels**. A second 1.3 Megapixel camera on the front can be used for video calling.

— copy ends —

Bluetoot: The Nokia Lumia 920 features 'Bluetooth 3.1', not 'Bluetoot'.

connectivty: 'connectivity'.

3G/HSPDA: Watch out for acronyms when they are used more than once in a sentence. A spell check will highlight all of the regardless and it can be easy to miss transposed letters. Here, 'HSDPA' (High-Speed Downlink Packet Access) is correct, but 'HSPDA' is incorrect. The Internet gives us an easy way to check on the correct spelling.

802.1a/b/g/n: Familiarity with the text or repetition of words can lull you into a false sense of security. In this case, it should be '802.11a/b/g/n' like the earlier reference. But the missing '1' isn't always easy to spot.

a 8.0 Megapixel: 'an 8.0 Megapixel...'

(with autofocus: Note the opening bracket here that doesn't have a corresponding closing bracket.

stablization: 'stabilisation' (British English) or

'stabilization' (US English)
  megapixels: 'Megapixels' has a capital 'M'.

Answers - 'Weather vane'

— copy starts —

He tried in **vane to fix the weather vane**. The blood pumped **through his vanes** as he banged the hammer down on the dented metal. "Must... Fix... The... Vane," he muttered. "He... Can't... Find... Out..." With each ear-splitting blow, the bent metal vane clattered and clanged on the old anvil. His dad would never understand. This was a **vane attempt** to avoid an argument. The new **iron ore vane** they'd discovered in the far field last week wouldn't keep him busy for long.

— copy ends —

vane to fix the weather vane: 'vain'. This excerpt tests your understanding of the homophones 'vane', 'vein' and 'vane'. They have the same pronunciation, but very different meanings.

through his vanes: 'veins'
vane attempt: 'vain'
iron ore vane: 'vein'

Answers - 'Star-spangled'

— copy starts —

O say can you see by the **dawns** early light,
What so proudly we hailed at the **twilights** last gleaming,
Whose broad stripes and bright stars through the perilous fight,
Oer the ramparts we watched, were so gallantly streaming
And the **rockets** red glare, the bombs bursting in air,
Gave proof through the night that our flag was still there;
O say does that star-spangled banner yet wave,
Oer the land of the free and the home of the **brave**
— copy ends —

dawns: The recognisable words to the 'Star-Spangled Banner' have been stripped of their apostrophes and question marks. So here, it should be 'dawn's'...

twilights: ... and here, it should be 'twilight's'.

Oer: The correct spelling is 'O'er', which is a shortened (and more poetic) version of 'over'.

streaming: There should be a question mark here - 'streaming?' It's the end of the sentence that poses the question: 'O say can you see...'

rockets: This should have an apostrophe after the 's' - 'rockets' red glare'.

Oer: Again, this should be 'O'er'.

brave: Like 'streaming' above, 'brave' needs to end with a question mark too. It ends the question started by the phrase 'O say does that star-spangled banner yet wave'. The full and corrected text follows:

O say can you see by the dawn's early light,
What so proudly we hailed at the twilight's last

gleaming,
    Whose broad stripes and bright stars through the perilous fight,
    O'er the ramparts we watched, were so gallantly streaming?
    And the rockets' red glare, the bombs bursting in air,
    Gave proof through the night that our flag was still there;
    O say does that star-spangled banner yet wave,
    O'er the land of the free and the home of the brave?

Answers - 'Penny Lane'

— copy starts —
In Penny Lane there is a barber showing photographs
Of every head he's had the pleasure to know.
And all the people that come and go,
Stop and say "hello".

On the corner is a banker with a motorcar,
The little children laugh at him behind his back.
And the banker never wears a mac,
In the pouring rain, very strange.

Penny Lane is in my ears and in my eyes.
There beneath the blue **surburban** skies
I sit, and meanwhile back

In Penny Lane there is a fireman with an hourglass.
And in his pocket is a portrait of the Queen.
He likes to keep his fire engine clean,
It's a clean machine.
— copy ends —

surburban: If you're familiar with the lyrics to this
classic Beatles song, then this familiarity might be a
hindrance when it comes to checking through the text for
errors. It's easy to get carried away by the content and not
see the words/spellings on the page. There's only one tiny
error in this text. It's an extra 'r' in 'suburban'.

Answers - 'The Manor'

— copy starts —

Come and see a **very unique** collaboration with students from Bucks New University. ***Sculpture in the Park*** is a series of large outdoor artworks inspired **by the the** history and surroundings of Hughenden Manor. From August to September, you can hear short talks from costumed characters **in costume** about what life was like at the house during the **mid-1800's**. Finally, if you're visiting us in December, enjoy the holiday season with atmospheric **victorian** show rooms decorated in traditional style. Plus there's plenty of family fun and ideas for **Christmas gifts!!**

— copy ends —

very unique: Look up the word 'unique' and the definition will read something like this: 'existing as the only one or as the sole example'. So something can't be 'very unique'. It is either 'unique' or it isn't.

***Sculpture in the Par*k**: The 'k' at the end of this phrase isn't italicised.

by the the: Double 'the'

in costume: Repetition. The characters are already 'costumed'

mid-1800's: This should read 'mid-1800s' - no apostrophe.

victorian: When describing the Victorian era, it has a capital 'V'.

Christmas gifts!!: An exclamation mark doesn't usually need to be used more than once, especially in more formal documents.

Answers - '30,000 trees'

— copy starts —

Ever since Hurricane **Catrina** battered New Orleans, the US Army Corps of Engineers has enforced vegetation removal on **levies** across the United States. But recent research has shown that trees can actually help to reinforce and strengthen these artificial walls. Consequently, the Corps has started to plant over 30,000 trees along the Sacramento River, as part of the $180 million **dollar** repairs to those **levies** that were overwhelmed by flooding. The Corps aims to do the planting over three months between December 2012 and **March 2012**. It will hire a contractor and does not yet have a cost estimate.

— copy ends —

Catrina: The Hurricane that hit New Orleans in 2005 was 'Katrina'.

levies: The correct spelling here is 'levees'. 'Levies' means 'amount owed' or 'conscripted troops', neither of which is suitable in this context.

dollar: Because there is already a dollar sign on '$180 million', there's no need to use the word 'dollar' here. Otherwise the phrase reads: '... as part of the 180 million dollar dollar repairs...'

levies: See above.

March 2012: This should be March 2013.

Answers - 'Texting'

We asked 100 London children how they communicate with their friends after school hours. Most admitted that they send texts or instant messages to their friends using their mobile phones. According to the survey, the **four principle** channels for this communication are: BlackBerry Messenger (BBM), Facebook and SMS messaging. **10** years ago this question would have **illicited** a very different response.

four: There are only 'three' channels mentioned in the following list

principle: 'principal'

10: The common way to write numbers is to spell out numbers one to nine as full words and write 10 and above in numerals. Starting a sentence with a number can also look ugly and isn't recommended.

illicited: 'Illicit' means 'illegal', so the word that should be used here is 'elicited', meaning 'to draw out'.

Answers - 'Boors'

— *copy starts* --
Can you believe it? We're going on a **boor hunt** today.
A **boor hunt**! They're wild pigs, I believe. It doesn't matter,
because I strongly disagree with this so-called 'sport' and I
don't like our host. I don't care if he does own half of
Oxfordshire. The man is relentlessly **borish**. In fact, the
whole weekend bores me. I'd much rather let the poor **boor**
roam free and spend my time at home with a good book.
— *copy ends* —

boor hunt: In this case it's 'boar hunt'. A 'boor' is a 'a
churlish, rude, or unmannerly person', a 'boar' is a 'wild
pig'. Going on a 'boor hunt', especially if you're carrying a
weapon, would be breaking the law.

borish: The correct spelling is 'boorish'.

boor: Again, 'boar'.

Answers - 'Quick snaps'

Most people take their digital cameras with them when they go on holiday or shoot quick snaps on **the mobile phones**. But, **more often then not**, the results can be **dissappointing**. This is **either** because most cameras aren't set up **correctly the subject** is poorly framed or the flash is set to Automatic when it should be **Disabled**. Fortunately, a few simple techniques can help you take better photos the next time you travel.

the mobile phones: A simple spelling mistake. It should read 'on their mobile phones'.

more often then not: The phrase should read 'more often than not'. It's easy to miss the incorrect word 'then', especially if you're familiar with the phrase. Your brain expects to see 'than' and often skips over the wrong word here because it looks similar.

dissappointing: The correct spelling of this word has a single 's' – 'disappointing'. A spell check should catch this error. But there are times when you won't have access to one.

either: While 'either' isn't spelt incorrectly here, it is being used incorrectly in this sentence. Why? Because it references three options – 'most cameras aren't set up correctly', 'the subject is poorly framed' and 'the flash is set to Automatic...' The definition of 'either' is 'one or the other of two people or things'. So it can't be followed by more than two things. It is 'either [something] or [something else]'. To fix this, we can either get rid of 'either' and leave the three options intact, or delete one of the three options and leave 'either' in place.

correctly the subject: There should be a comma between 'correctly' and 'the subject'.

Disabled: In this instance, there's no capital D in 'disabled'. It's not a camera function, like Automatic.

Answers - 'Murder'

— copy starts —

"Yes, I was on the trip to **south** America, as **was** Mr Carmichael and Doctor Jarratt. Why do you ask?"

The policeman flipped open his notebook. "Did you happen to meet a Mr Jonathan Hart at any point?"

"Actually, yes. He dined at our table on our first night at **see**. He worked for an oil company, I think. Why do you **ask?".**

"Because Mr Hart was murdered," said the policeman flatly. "And you were one of the last people to see him alive."

"You have a **flare** for the dramatic, officer. What can I do to help?"

— copy ends —

south: This should be capped as it's referencing the region – 'South America'.

was: Because there are two people being referenced here – 'Mr Carmichael' and 'Doctor Jarratt' – we need to use 'were' instead of 'was'.

see: This should, of course, be 'sea'.

ask?".: Did you spot the unnecessary full stop at the end of this sentence? Because there's already a question mark here, there's no need for one.

flare: The correct word should be 'flair'. 'Flare' typically means 'a sudden brief burst of bright flame or light'. The policeman might light a flare every time he's being dramatic, but it's highly doubtful.

Answers - 'Ooh, oh, ah'

— copy starts —

Before every **convert** performance, Zack warms up his vocal **chords** with a series of simple singing exercises. The idea is to relax his throat and release any built-up tension in the muscles. He says that his routine hasn't changed since his first appearance at the Royal Albert Hall. He starts with some neck rolls, followed by a series of shoulder rolls, before launching into a gentle set of half-scales using vowel sounds ("ooh", "oh", **"ah'**, "ee" and "eh").

— copy ends —

convert: concert
chords: cords
"ah': There's a missing quotation mark here. It should be written "ah".

Answers - 'Frost'

— copy starts —

Richard Frost was at the peak of his physical fitness and his excellent racing results had **peaked** the interest of the national cycling coach. On the Thursday after Easter, the coach decided to take a **peak** at Richard's punishing training regime, which involved a challenging mountain peak climb, followed by a fast descent into the valley below.

— copy ends —

peaked: This should be 'piqued'.

peak: This should be 'peek'. It's easy to get the homophones 'peek', 'peak' and 'pique' confused.

7. Appendix (and other stuff)

The majority of today's communication still uses the written word. So whether you're publishing an article or a book, writing a report or putting up a sign, it's important to get those words right. As we've seen, there are many ways to make mistakes and the methods we use to try and spot them are far from perfect. But by getting to know the mistakes that we commonly make, why we make them, and why we might not spot them, we can try to improve our publishing accuracy.

Proofreading is an almost impossible job. You won't spot everything. Professional proofreaders don't spot everything. If they did, then professionally published content wouldn't have any spelling slip-ups or grammar goofs. And it does. But by building a proofreading stage into content publishing, you can hope to minimise mistakes, even eradicate them completely. Use the methods and checklists in this book and pay particular attention to titles, subheadings and anything that will be shown in a large text size.

You CAN proofread your own work. But I won't lie to you, it's not easy. There's a familiarity that you have with what you've written that's difficult to erase. But if you can get some distance between you and your work and reformat it so that it looks and feels new, you can get a new perspective on your content. That said, it's still a good idea to get somebody else to look over your work before you finish it. This is especially important if you are printing anything. In fact, I'd say it's vital. That way you can elevate yourself above the people who thought that a train station poster saying: 'I love the scenary around Watergate Bay...' was error-free.

By knowing what to look for, you can dramatically improve your proofreading skills. By questioning everything you see, you can dramatically improve your proofreading skills. By giving content an extra read-through, just to be sure, you can... You guessed it - dramatically improve your proofreading skills.

This book covers a lot of ground. But if there's anything that didn't get covered sufficiently or there's any other aspect of proofreading or copy editing that you'd like more information on, drop me an email at **dean@goodcontentcompany.com** and I'll consider adding it for free to the Good Content Company website.

Thanks for reading.

Style guide template

A style guide can help you enforce consistency in content that you publish as part of a brand. But how do you go about putting one together? You can take inspiration from the AP Stylebook, used by the newspaper industry in the US. Or the Yahoo! Style Guide, which is effectively the AP Stylebook for web content. Use these as a foundation for building your own customised and personalised style guide. You'll find umpteen links to them (and to organisations that have used them) online.

The key thing to remember is that your style guide doesn't need to be exhaustive from the get-go. You can add to it as you encounter stylistic/tonal inconsistencies in your content. In the meantime, here's a simple template we made earlier...

Step 1: Define your target audience

Know who you're writing for, their level of knowledge about your subject and what they like/don't like. A short paragraph will suffice. Take a look at this short example from a music magazine that I worked on: "the readership varies from aspiring 16-year-old metal guitarists to octogenarian viola players, reflecting a spread of gender, class and political leaning. As such, we can never assume that the readers will understand the same musical/cultural references or in-jokes."

Step 2: Set the style & tone

Define how do you want to sound to your readers. What's your voice like? Chatty and informal? Or more straight-laced and authoritative? Can you write in the first person? Can you use slang words? How much jargon is too much jargon? Take a look at this overview of style and tone from another company that I freelanced for: "We celebrate the extraordinary, the wonderful, the unique, the local.

Never be grey or mundane. Tell stories, give examples, add colour, avoid bland and corporate... Be human, warm, occasionally funny - and use 'I' and 'we'..."

Step 3: Describe the formatting

In this section, briefly describe your preferred formatting options so that they can be consistent across everything you create, edit and publish. These might include:

- How you write abbreviations
- Whether you use accents on words
- The format of captions, straps, headlines and subheadings
- Whether captions have full stops
- How you write dates, times, weights & measurements, numbers, percentages, fractions, telephone numbers, money, email and web addresses
- How you format bullet/numbered lists
- What fonts you use
- When you should use italics/bold
- When you capitalise words
- Preferred image sizes
- How links are shown

Each section might look like this:

DATES
Dates should be written as follows:
27 September 2013
26-27 September 2013
September 2013
21st century, 50th anniversary, 1990s

ITALICS

The title of the publication/brand should always be italicised.

All media publications, such as films, games, books and music titles should also be italicised. I.e. *The LA Times*, *Star Wars*, *The Catcher In The Rye*.

Step 4: Nail down the grammar

Describe key punctuation rules, such as use of semi-colons, apostrophes and any brand-specific rules (like using single quote marks instead of traditional quote marks), whether you use ampersands and whether you use exclamation marks. Format these rules as above. For example:

BRACKETS

Use square brackets where adding an editorial explanation into reported speech. I.e. In a quote that reads: "Michael believed that he was to blame", you could clarify the 'he' reference if it is not immediately obvious who it refers to. So the sentence could be tweaked to say: "Michael believed that [his father] was to blame."

FULL STOPS

Always include a full stop at the end of all straps and pull quotes. There's no full stop at the end of headers, captions or bullet/numbered lists.

Step 5: Common spelling mistakes/rules

This section of a style guide is usually a mix of common spelling errors and a glossary that explains words and abbreviations that are specific to the brand or publication. It might also contain words that you do not want to use in your content and whether you use British or US English spellings. Arrange these in alphabetical order for easy reference. For example:

E

Email - one word, no hyphen

Elicit is to 'draw out or bring out'. Illicit means 'illegal or not permitted'

F

Facebook – upper case F

filmmaker – all one word, no hyphen

far East – but Middle East

Step 6: Define the content structure

Your style guide can also specify rules for particular content types - news, features, interviews, and so on. This might include overall word counts, required elements (i.e. header, body copy, image captions, fact box...) and word counts for those elements (i.e. header, 20 words max; body copy, 400 words max, etc).

Copy editing checklist

Assume everything is wrong
Keep an original version of the text for reference

- Read through copy without changing anything - don't run a spell check
- Make notes of any errors that jump out
- Is the copy what you want? Does it fulfil the brief or commission?
- Does it include all the necessary elements? (header, strap, body copy that fits word count, captions, etc)
- Does it all make sense?
- Does the copy flow or does it ramble? Be on the lookout for: overlong or fragmented sentences, overlong paragraphs, poor word choice (keep it simple), style guide clashes, word repetition, word consistency, tense-switching, cliches/overused words or phrases, unexplained jargon or acronyms
- Does it start too slowly/have a good hook?
- Is the content too long? Or too short?
- Are the facts correct? (places, people, products, email addresses, web URLs, etc)
- Is the spelling correct?
- Is the grammar correct?
- Is anything offensive/libellous?

Always re-read a sentence that you've edited
Re-read the content at the end of the editing process and, ideally, leave some time before proofreading

Proofreading checklist

Assume there are errors
Keep an original version of the text for reference
Have the right tools to hand
Work in a comfortable environment
Minimise distractions

- Read slowly - try tapping each word to reduce reading speed. Or use one of these tactics below:
- Print the content out and edit with a red pen
- Search for different errors on multiple read-throughs
- Change how the content looks - increase the font, change the device you're using to read it or try changing the software to alter the formatting
- Read the content backwards
- Read the content aloud
- Check for spelling errors and inconsistencies
- Check for missing words
- Check for words that don't adhere to the style guide*
- Check punctuation is correct (consider pacing and rhythm)
- Check punctuation adheres to the style guide*
- Check formatting (double spaces, misaligned paragraphs, etc)
- Check for missing text elements (subheadings, captions, etc)
- Check references are correct (i.e. 'See page 53')
- Check images (if applicable)
- Check page numbers (if applicable)

Always re-read a sentence that you've edited
Run a spell check

Re-read the content at the end of the proofreading process as a final error-check

Interested in proofreading symbols? Find the standard squiggles at www.chicagomanualofstyle.org/tools_proof.html.

*Not always applicable

Dean Evans? Who he?

Since 1992, Dean Evans has written hundreds of thousands of words from technology news and movie reviews to celebrity interviews and books (like this one). Dean is the founder of The Good Content Company, which currently provides copywriting/freelance writing services and time-saving content creation tools. He lives in the UK with his wife, two children and a work-in-progress novel about wizards.

Connect with Dean at:
www.goodcontentcompany.com/about
twitter.com/goodcontentco
twitter.com/evansdp

There's More Where This Came From

Want to make all aspects of content creation easier and faster? Check out the FREE creative tools at:
www.goodcontentcompany.com/tools

Other books by The Good Content Company

The Good Content Code
Write Great Headlines Every Time

For more information about writing, editing and proofreading, join the Good Content Company mailing list at: www.goodcontentcompany.com

Got 5 minutes? Please leave a review

If this book has helped you in any way, it would be fantastic if you could support us by leaving a review on Amazon saying what you found useful, how the information helped you and what you liked the most. You can also give it a thumbs-up by clicking 'Like' on its Amazon book page. We'd appreciate that too. A lot.

A positive review helps independent publishers like us to get our books found on Amazon's infinite virtual shelves. Reviews also help us to improve on what we do and how we do what we do. The more books we sell, the more we can concentrate on developing new tools to help creative people like you work faster and smarter.

Thanks in advance.

Credits

1. 'Salt and freshly ground black people' -
http://www.theprooffairy.com/blogging/3-examples-of-
why-proofreading-is-so-important/
2. King James Bible -
http://news.bbc.co.uk/1/hi/uk/2368997.stm
3. 'Laeping to literacy' -
http://www.happyplace.com/3761/the-best-spelling-
mistakes-on-education-related-signs
4. The Guardian Corrections and Clarifications -
http://www.guardian.co.uk/theguardian/series/correctionsan
dclarifications
5. Ohio State University -
http://researchnews.osu.edu/archive/multitask.htm
6. Science Now -
http://news.sciencemag.org/sciencenow/2010/04/multitaski
ng-splits-the-brain.html
7. Physorg.com - http://phys.org/news/2011-04-eyes-
brain.html
8. Matt Davis - http://www.mrc-
cbu.cam.ac.uk/people/matt.davis/cmabridge/
9. Libel - http://legal-
dictionary.thefreedictionary.com/libel
10. Excerpt from Guardian Style -
http://image.guardian.co.uk/sys-
files/Guardian/documents/2007/12/11/guardianstylebook20
07.pdf
11. Cornell University/Alan Hedge -
http://ergo.human.cornell.edu/Conferences/EECE_IEQ%20
and%20Productivity_ABBR.pdf
12. Fast Company -
http://www.fastcompany.com/3001316/want-more-
productive-workers-adjust-your-thermostat

Printed in Great Britain
by Amazon

30634524R00097